Run to Win:
The Mongoose System
Coaching Middle School & Youth Basketball

Beau James Brock, Karen Recurt Kyler, L. Thomas Szekely

ISBN: 978-1-4834-0882-8 (sc)
ISBN: 978-1-4834-0881-1 (e)

Cover photo by Lorin Caruso

Lulu Publishing Services rev. date: 02/18/2014

Contents

— ◼ —

HELLO 2016 BLAINE BOYS BASKETBALL COMMUNITY!!!

Coach John and I are expecting this to be an extremely fun season. As a **"Basketball Community"**, we will be doing things a bit differently from years past. JV and Varsity will both run the same exciting, **up-tempo "Mongoose System"** – think early 90's LMU. Statistics prove that **the team that shoots more wins**, and we plan on shooting a whole lot. As such, the JV and Varsity will mostly practice together as one community. This will also present many **opportunities to rotate JV players to play with their Varsity** brothers (both figuratively and literally) **on Saturday** Game Days.

PRACTICES will be on **TUES/THURS** from **4:15 to 6:00p.**

THERE WILL BE NO JV GAME THIS WEEKEND.

If you will **NOT** be **AVAILABLE FOR** any **GAME**, please **LET US KNOW** by the **THURSDAY** practice before said game.

PARENTS Volunteers are **NEEDED** for both JV and Varsity games **TO CHART SHOOTING STATS.** Please let me know if you are interested.

Any questions, feel free to send me an email @ cmfontenot1@yahoo.com.

THANKS.... And **GOOOO TIGERS! RRROOOAAARRR!**
/Coach Christian.
(cell) 225-281-4234

Book Dedication

---■---

Coach Tommy:

I would like to dedicate this book to my father. You taught me things in life that I could never learn from any book and the best part is that you never really had to say a word. You were a great role model and a wonderful father, the very reason I take so much joy in coaching. You will always be with me. I would also like to dedicate this book to my two daughters, Katelyn and Madison, without the love I share with the two of you I would only be a fraction of the person I am today. Your understanding of my passion and commitment to give back to others allows me to do what I enjoy. To the two of you I say thank you.

2 Timothy 4:7

I have fought the good fight, I have finished
the race, I have kept the faith.

Coach Karen:

I want to dedicate this book to my family (especially my husband) for allowing me the opportunity to spend so much time away from home! To my daughter Kandace, who gave me the greatest joy, of coaching her this past year in four different league seasons. Also, I'd like to thank Coach Beau for picking me to be the SRK, CD and GM!

(Shot Record Keeper, Correspondence Director and General Manager) I truly enjoyed working with you and Coach Tommy especially when I taught you to duck, whenever I wanted to shoot you, both!!! But, mainly Beau ;-)

And finally, to our special group of girls, with their hard work and dedication to this team this journey would not have been possible.

Coach Beau:

I want to dedicate this book to my dad who was my first coach and taught me the love of the game, and ignited my torch of competition which I burn to teach others to live. I love you, dad. I also want to dedicate this book to Coach Chuck Scanlon, the "John Wooden of Minnesota soccer" who just retired after 30 years of successful teaching and coaching at Apple Valley Senior High, who taught me leadership and commitment to the team, first and always. He gave me my proudest moment as a player in sport, the opportunity to carry <u>him</u> off the field, in victory. Finally, to my three sons, who I hope will share my love of sport and the possibilities it holds, for the rest of their lives.

Purpose

— ■ —

This book has been written to teach you how to coach the *System* to middle school and youth basketball teams. Other books on the *System* have been organized for college and high school level teams, and we wanted to provide the lessons we have happily learned to you for your kids at the middle school level. <u>We have written this book for you</u>. You picked this book up because no matter how much you already know about basketball, you know there is more to learn. If you are a parent or teacher just starting out in coaching, you have picked this up to *begin* to learn to coach. If you have already coached for 5 years, you may be looking for a new approach to the game. If you have coached 10 years or more, you know that the more you know about the game, the more there is to learn.

In any case, the opportunity to coach young men and women is the opportunity, to not only teach them how the game is played, but how the game itself teaches life lessons which are portable skills they can and will use for the rest of their lives. Your mission as their coach, is to provide these young people with the right lessons. In the over 30 years of combined coaching among us, we have found nothing "new under the sun", but in the quest for providing those in our charge with the best possible opportunity to learn, compete and win, we have developed our philosophy we call, the **Mongoose System.** Like every coaching staff before us we have taken the lessons from all those who came before us, we have adapted those lessons through trial and experience, and decided to set down for you a basketball philosophy that can provide your players, their parents, and your school or club team with the most significant team learning experience we think possible in the game, today.

The modern *System* offense was made famous by Paul Westhead and LMU and then used successfully for years at Grinnell College, in Iowa, and other schools. We combine this non-stop attacking style of play with the life lessons made famous by John Wooden and his Pyramid of Success as the core of our teaching. We will present the **Mongoose System** in components and you can learn and then teach it in stages so as to not overwhelm your players. In many ways, the **Mongoose System** is designed to be a "Lombardi-esque" type of game philosophy which encourages fundamentals first, execution second, and grit third. Your players, no matter their base ability, will improve using this philosophy and will only love the game, even more.

Introduction

■

Now, our basketball teams **run to win**. We all started out coaching with playing style we grew up playing, a half court offensive game - breaking only when necessary, and with switching half court man to man defense and pressing only when behind. It slowed the game down for the kids and was the easiest to "control" from the sidelines as coach. We had success coaching this way though and focused on fundamentals and team discipline on both offense and defense and looking to Coach John Wooden as a guide and his model of play, and most importantly his Pyramid of Success for life lessons.

A few years ago, in the spring of 2010, we saw a video that changed how we coached young people, ***Guru of Go***. It was the story of Paul Westhead and the Loyola Marymount (LMU) college basketball team and the late Hank Gathers. Frankly, it was an epiphany. It opened our eyes to the possibility of how we could make the game more fun, maximize the talents of our best players, and at the same time, provide our players whose skills were not as developed, the opportunity to provide more value to the team <u>and</u> dramatically elevate their own self-confidence. All of these positives added up to one thing, if we figured out how to the run the ***System*** for this level, we would exponentially increase the players' <u>love of the game itself</u>, and this would in turn make them be more hungry to learn and improve, both at formal practice and at home in their driveway.

We then tried to learn as much as we could about the **System**, and discovered so much information that we were ashamed that we had been so ignorant of its implementation at schools, like Grinnell College under Coach Dave Arsenault, since the mid-90's. We bought and studied the video made by Paul Westhead from the '90's at LMU and then Dave Arseneault videos. Next, we were overjoyed by the publishing of the bible on the **System** in 2011 that we literally carried around with our Bible RSV, *Coaching the System: A Complete Guide to Basketball's Most Explosive Style of Play* by Coach Gary Smith and Coach Doug Porter. All of these videos and publications focused on college and varsity high school teams and even openly dissuaded its utilization at lower levels of play, although they proffered a mathematical model of success if put into use.

For the past two years straight we have organized, practiced and competed using our own version we have called the **Mongoose System**, which we believe is not only a possible way to coach middle school and youth basketball, but the optimum way to coach at this level. The **Mongoose System** places all the lessons from innovative trailblazers like Wooden, Westhead, Arseneault, Smith & Porter into our own gumbo and we season it generously in classic Louisiana tradition. As you are aware, most middle school and youth players do not play high school ball, and the opportunity to teach this love of the game and fundamentals, to all of these young people can be done successfully and by using it, you will make a difference in their lives.

And what price would you pay to change your child's life for the better? What is the most important thing in your life more than your family? What if you could make that same positive difference in the lives of not only your child, but countless others? This is the difference you make when you are a positive coach, a role model and mentor for young people as they are confronted by unknown challenges through sport, which then serve to define their strength and character.

We all have been blessed with the opportunity to coach our own children and the children of others and this grave responsibility is one we have decided is worth every minute of struggle which has been and continues to run the full gamut of life experiences.

Coaching middle school and youth basketball can be full of enormous challenges, from coaching your own child to being responsible for the development of 8 to 10 young people who look to you for guidance, leadership and support. Nine of whom, you probably did not get to choose to be on your team, and even if you did, they are unfamiliar with what you say, the how you say things, and even what in the wide wide world of sports you mean, when you do say things.

The **Mongoose System** is designed to be taught in programs, increasing in difficulty, depending on the age and skill of your players, the number of players you have to put on the court and the amount of practice time you have available to you. The programs of **Mongoose System** development are Mercury, Gemini and Apollo. With Mercury, your team can launch itself off the pad and compete with the System with limited players and limited practice time regardless of base ability. As you progress to Gemini, you will need a team of nine to ten players, and your team will then implement additional full court pressure defenses, out of bounds plays, and more complex rotational shifts. When you are ready to advance to Apollo, you will need to know your players and their abilities. In order to be successful at

Apollo, you need to be able to field ten to fifteen players. Your practice time commitment must be significant early in pre-season and it will involve the introduction of all the concepts and demands of the **Mongoose System**. If you teach the Apollo program to your middle school team, they can reach the moon as you remove all restraints on their talent and unleash "organized chaos."

CHAPTER 1

—————————— ■ ——————————

Mongoose System Philosophy

The foundation of this philosophy is that all players have value and can contribute to the team's success. Some may be excellent shooters, some at setting picks, some passers, some rebounders, and others as defensive stand outs. Every player must be supportive of his or her teammates especially when they make mistakes. It is not enough to be positive when winning, it is he mark of a champion as to what her or his attitude is when persevering through adversity. *Some days you eat the bear, and some days the bear eats you.* Players must come prepared to play and give 100% at <u>each</u> practice and <u>each</u> game. Each player chooses how hard they will work. A coach can motivate, but not compel performance and she or he will not be able to trap on defense, rebound any balls nor shoot a single basket.

The team will learn the whole, and then the parts of the **Mongoose System**, and teaching basketball skills will be done in conjunction with teaching life skills from the Wooden Pyramid of Success. The players will be taught that each trip down the court is a new and separate life, and the previous trips are to be forgotten. This is because there will be mistakes, there will be turnovers, and these cannot be the players' nor your focus as coach. Correct what you can, quickly, simply, and without elevating the players of anxiety. The players must <u>know</u> they are free to perform their role in this "dance" and not hesitate to execute on their training. We will rotate as many players on and off the floor, <u>every minute</u>, restricted only by roster size or local league rules. Team goals are the paramount interests in the players' minds and we use the modified Grinnell System goals for elementary or junior high levels of play:

Middle School: 45S + 22 3's + 33% OR + 12 SD + 16 TO's = Win

Elementary: 30S + 15 3's + 33% OR + 8 SD + 10 TO's = Win

This means at the middle school level we are attempting 45 shots, half which are 3 pointers, rebound 1/3 of our missed shots from the floor, shoot 12 more times than our opponents, and force 16 turnovers by our opponents.

On offense we will attempt to take a shot within twelve seconds of getting control of the ball, we run all the time, and not hold anything, we run to win. We will have a preferred shooter order in which the point guard acts as the floor general and she or he makes the decision at full speed to whom to distribute the ball based on a defined order of progressions. The receiver then looks to shoot the ball, immediately, from where they are on the floor or drive to the basket if overplayed by the defender. As Westhead puts it, the point guard is passing for a shot. Everyone shoots. Everyone drives with a cross-over move when overplayed and unable to shoot from their "spot." Everyone rebounds except for the assigned safety valve on the court.

On defense, everyone runs all the time. Each player creates pressure but also space between himself or herself and our opponent who has the ball UNTIL they pick it up and then our player "rips their face off." We will run the highest pressure full court or half court defense the local league rules allow. We will trap everywhere on the court, all the time.

Everyone must be prepared to press after a made basket and in half court be prepared to rotate to the ball with half court pressing "attack" if forced to withdraw from full court pressure. Everyone must keep their hands and arms moving all the time and interrupt the passing lanes during this pressure even more than their teammates who are defending on-ball. We are looking for steals and turnovers all the time and our safety, in our press, <u>must not</u> give up any layups or shots from the block when our opponents break our press, which will happen even when your players are giving 100%. Shots from other locations remarkably reduce opponents FG% at this level of play, and the rest of your players will then be able to recover and assist in getting the rebound and then resuming an immediate assault back up the court in transition.

In establishing who will play where on your team, here are the roles and responsibilities by position each player must fulfill:

- **Player 1 – Point Guard**
  - *The 1 is a leader. He or she must be unselfish in the distribution of the ball. He or she must be able to penetrate and look basket first. She or he must motivate their teammates with positive reinforcement and maintain the highest basketball I.Q. on the squad.*

o 1 drills focus on every angle of lane penetration, 3 point jump stop shooting & passing to multiple options.

o On defense, the 1 may be a trapper, an interceptor, or play off-ball denial depending on the particular press defense being played.

- **Player 2 – Shooting Guard**

    o The 2 is fearless in shooting from outside the arch whenever open. He or she works on offense with a "Closer" mentality, *forgetting every missed shot*, and be willing to drive hard to the basket if and when the defense comes out and overplays. The 2 becomes the QB after receiving the ball but must always be indoctrinated with the progression ingrained in their mind to: (1) shoot; (2) drive; and if not (1) or (2) then (3) pass to other options.

    o 2 drills focus on 3 point shots from his or her "spot" and penetration techniques from the wing.

    o On defense, the 2 is primarily an interceptor in the press.

- **Player 3 – Small Forward**

    o The 3 is the team cheetah and makes layups and shots from the block without fail. She or he must run the floor at a sprinter's pace (NEVER JOG) in their lane. The 3 must execute cutting to the ball & picks with a razor's precision.

    o 3 drills focus on layups and controlling long (and sometimes erratic) passes from the 1 off fast breaks and picks.

    o On defense, the 3 is our best trapper and sets up on our opponents' ball handler's strong side, i.e – the left side vs. a right hander, and forcing the ball handler to work to their weaker hand never allowing them to get to the sideline first.

- **Player 4 – Power Forward**
  - The 4 has the heart of a lion on offense. She or he must run the floor every time knowing their primary role in the **Mongoose System** is to provide a last option as a shooter in the primary fast break and to be a screener in the secondary break. The 4 must be hungry for rebounds and go directly to the basket to grab and quickly put it back in or be willing to kick it back out to the 2 for another 3 point shot. If he or she does receive the ball, they must be able to quickly pivot and release the ball from the elbow on the court.
  - 4 drills focus on pick/roll and rebounding. Also, catching long and intermediate passes and pivoting for quick releases.
  - On defense, the 4 is a primary trapper, along with the 3, in full court and must be aggressive in closing the trap without "overplaying" and allowing our opponent's ball handler cut back and escape the vortex of the trap.

- **Player 5 – Center**
  - The 5 is the Zulu warrior on offense. She or he will be fearless in aggressive rebounding from the center of the paint every time down the floor and lead the team in offensive rebounding. The 5 must be the most athletic player combining strength and courage under the basket and proficient in the pick and roll. The 5 is also best to be the second most cerebral on the team as the 5 throws the ball in after our opponents score and in our press breaks and cannot be

mentally fragile under this pressure. The 5 also is a 3 point shooter from the top of the key.

- 5 drills focus on pick/roll, rebounding, second jump rebounding, strong drives inside the paint, and 3 point shots. Also, 2 on 1 defensive drills as the 5 working as the safety.
- On defense, the 5 is the safety in our presses and must <u>not</u> allow layups and be aggressive in looking to intercept the bomb pass.

CHAPTER 2

■

Why you are here

You are a Middle School AD or basketball coach

You are a Middle School Athletic Director or basketball coach. The parents of your school expect you success on the court by your teams and a healthy and vigorous competitive spirit by all your teams. The parents expect you to educate and challenge their children to reach new levels of skill and development in mind and body under your tutelage.

I tell you fervently, the **Mongoose System** is the way. A commitment is not even required by all three grades at your school for an investment of this philosophy to be successful. However, the greater the planting, the greater the reaping at harvest time will be. The time spent, rather than on complicated offensive schemes, but instead on fundamentals, team discipline and execution will dramatically improve your program. If coaching at your program can be organized to all incorporate this philosophy we believe it will create immediate tangible improvements and results.

Your players will individually be able to improve, from their own level of skill to the next, regardless of whether they are novice or expert at the game due to the simplification of the tasks you will now be asking them to execute. They will bond as a team like never before as they all, will and must, play without abandon on the court for it to be successful and will demand the highest commitment not just from themselves but others on the team. They will know you are unleashing their abilities and removing the restrictions anyone before placed on their potential. The history of Western Civilization is clear that twelve people can change the world BUT they must receive the correct lesson, become inspired, and evangelize the lesson through deed.

Your parents will be reinvigorated through the process in watching the elevated confidence and athleticism of their children. And finally, the full implementation of the **Mongoose System** will provide excitement from tip-off to final horn for your student body to stand behind and cheer. It all begins with a team. A team where every person on it has a defined and specially important role for its success, and this philosophy demands all the players contribute by performing their role to the hilt.

You are a Parent

If you are here because you are a parent, get ready for one of the most difficult challenges you will have to experience. This is because the "filter" on communication that exists between you and someone else's child and vice versa does <u>not</u> exist when it comes to your own child. If your child is highly manipulative before you began coaching him or her, and all children manipulate to a degree, this behavior will be magnified beginning probably with the first practice. You must set guidelines inside your family home about how you will be the coach <u>only</u> at practice and the games and not the parent, and that you will treat your child like every other child without favoritism or greater criticism.

We have found it helps if your child is either the very best on the team or the least skilled, but rarely is that the case, and nepotism as to position or playing time will be entirely counterproductive to your child's development and team bonding so you need to be overtly aware of this potential scenario. And then, avoid it! Our best suggestion is to have another coach on your team handle as much of the direct one on one instruction of your child as possible and then after practice, do your best to let it go at the gym and <u>not</u> bring home what happened there.

Sure, work with him or her at home in the driveway when you can, but put your mom or dad hat back on when there to maintain a safe normalizing relationship within your home. Your child needs to feel home is "base" and safe no matter how stressful practice or games may be, because always keep in mind no matter how much pressure you place on them to succeed, they already are wanting to impress <u>you</u> as well as everyone else more than you will ever know. That's the inherent pressure that is placed on <u>them</u> when you choose to be their coach.

You played before

Congratulations, perhaps you played before when you were younger, maybe at a high level of college or top high school varsity level and now you are coaching 8-14 year old children. Sometimes, the better you are as an athlete, however, the harder it can be to understand and be patient with coaching, John Wooden being a notable exception to this rule. The difficulty can be with this experience for you to take the time to learn, how to teach. Obviously, you are taking care to do this right now and your efforts are to be applauded as you cannot get a "do over" with a particular group of young people once you engage with them.

Just remember, even Ted Williams, the greatest hitter of all time and had 20/10 vision, had grave difficulty managing a baseball team because he couldn't understand and communicate effectively how to develop his players and deal with losses through this process. I point this out because Williams was not only the greatest hitter, but also a clubhouse leader as a player and a highly successful Marine pilot in both World War II and Korea, and so you'd expect he would have also been a great baseball manager.

The **Mongoose System** provides you with a game philosophy that streamlines this obstacle your playing experience may present to effective coaching by minimizing time you need to spend on overall strategy and allows you the time to spend with players on fundamentals. It allows you to organize your team by skill level, quickly assign them to positions, and develop the patience to teach them individually.

You have coached a long time

If you have coached a long time you are already a successful role model for children, period. Whether you have 1000 wins, 500 wins or 100 wins to your coaching resume, you know it's the wins in the development of young hearts and minds with the spirit of competition and perseverance that count.

The **Mongoose System** will give you the flexibility to integrate your tried and true coaching methods to this philosophy of play by simplifying both offense and defense and allow you to focus on what you already do best, development of skills and motivational playing techniques. It will also expand your tool kit in dealing with teams you may have had the luxury to remain with for more than a season or two and elevate them to the next level of competitive greatness.

You run a youth sports organization

You run the local sports program and your primary goal is to educate and provide the athletic opportunity for more and more children and grow your program. We believe the **Mongoose System** will help provide the answer to reach both those goals especially in circumstances when practice times are limited and at a premium. It will make the game more fun for the players. It will maximize participation for your parents who want to see their child on the floor. It gives a model for all your coaches in your program to simplify offensive schemes. Finally, it lays the foundation for player development and focus on what the middle school and high school in your area truly want, the fundamental skills which will be portable for the players to take to the their level.

Many youth programs require a minimum amount of play for its players with some even mandating "equal" playing time and this philosophy will meet that requirement and then some. It does so by providing guidance to its program's coaches to teach their players the whole scheme first, one program at a time, and then the parts, when the greatest individual player development occurs. Only then after the team understands their roles and can perform together, an advance is made to the next programmatic level, e.g. Mercury to Gemini.

CHAPTER 3

■

The System works

Run to win. Not mine, again, but St. Paul's from his letter to the Corinthians. Isn't everything in the Bible? At least that's what my Baptist grandma taught me, even though I was raised Catholic by my parents. And so, it gave me great comfort when I was watching (and later made my teams watch) the NFL Films classic video "Lombardi" originally aired in 1968. In it, Coach Lombardi reached into the Bible for inspiration for the Packers during a critical stretch of his, what now seems to have been fated by someone above, three consecutive NFL Championship run. Run to win. We even made book marks for our team and laminated them at the local copy shop to reinforce the lesson:

Do you not know that all the runners in a stadium compete, but only one receives the prize? So run to win.

1 Corinthians 9:24

By playing the **Mongoose System** in the middle school and youth levels, your team will be dictating the pace of the game and your team will feel in more in control whereas your opponents will feel hurried, anxious and disorganized. It does create an "organized chaos" on the floor to <u>your</u> advantage when your players continue to move.

Lightning warfare isn't a new concept. It's not a 20th century concept, just ask the Mongols. But in basketball, this lightning warfare allows for maximum dividends in several areas of the game. First, it deprives your opponents the chance to set up a structured offense. By trapping all the way down the court, you force your opponents to find alternative methods for advancing the ball up the court and then attack your basket from different launch points which only add to their confusion. Our philosophy for middle school and youth teams differs from some of the other **System** gospels, which we have the highest respect for, by normally playing off the in-bounds thrower and with two basic full court presses until the team reaches the Apollo program level of proficiency.

Next, the **Mongoose System** wears out your opponents as they will most likely to playing the minimum number of players and keeping their best five players on the court as much as possible. At the middle school level, teams generally have one, or maybe two, top ball handlers and your trapping pressure will both physically and mentally wear this player down, and can frequently frustrate him or her until they personally break. And as we know, if the head of the snake is cut off, then the snake dies.

Third, your opponents will be unable to press for fear of wearing out their players by running a full court game against your team. Although many times we would like a team to press us because once we break it we are ideally built to run the fast break, it also will allow you to place your secondary ball handler at the 1, a player who may <u>not</u> be the ideal candidate to carry the ball up the court through a press. By obtaining this advantage, you then may move your "primary 1" to a spot where she or he can provide your team with another shooting weapon.

When your opponent is confused, they become demoralized. Napoleon teaches us that morale is 3x as important as physical capability. We have found that our opponents can be so dazed and tired during the first half by the relentless pressure, it is not until halftime that they become demoralized because they finally got a few minutes to realize what happened to them and that now they are in for another half of it! Also, coaches at this level want to have their players try something different, "make the adjustment" at half, which many players are unable to perform at the same level of proficiency as their regular offense or defense they predominantly have practiced and thus when that fails, morale sinks further into the abyss.

This pressure creates high anxiety on your opponents' bench. And I mean on your opponents' coaches! Whatever plan they had for their boys or girls, that plan will now have to change. Most teams at this level focus their practice time on a one or two offensive sets or set plays in a half court game. They will work on a couple of presses and press breaks, and when fatigued, they will make mistakes, and we all know how fast turnovers can add up to points. The anxiety is only heightened by the full five person rotation you will implement especially if your opponents are playing man to man defense as they will have to find their "new" mark every minute. Also, their coach will become frustrated with these turnovers and even more so when their team begins to miss easy shots due to being fatigued. Because this is another benefit of your players running to win, rotating every minute, pressure all the way down the court, and your opponents not substituting their bench in kind.

Tactically, this trapping and pressure is designed to take your opponents' best player out of the game and make the other players beat you. On many teams, they are built around a single threat and structure their offense around that threat. The **Mongoose System** is fundamentally designed to disrupt that scheme so common at middle school and youth basketball. If you have an AAU team, then your personnel is much deeper and so is you opponents, but the logic remains true as to fatigue.

So let's stop cursing the darkness and light a candle! The **Mongoose System** emphasizes athleticism, but you don't need ten "Amazons" or ten Presidential Fitness Award winners to be successful. You <u>need</u> eight to ten, with ten being the best number (with 5 or 6 minute stopped time quarters at this level) young people who want to compete. You need players who want to part of something bigger than themselves, and are willing to play with reckless abandon. It emphasizes team "dance," in that, off-ball movement becomes more important than on-ball, and everyone is moving and participating on every play during the minute they are on the court. They must not stop moving as the energy they exert serves to drain your opponents as none of it is wasted motion.

Finally, the **Mongoose System** emphasizes personal courage and commitment regardless of size and strength. Your players are required to believe in themselves and their teammates in order for this to work and while on the court on offense they will, to paraphrase Coach Wooden, be quick to the spot, but don't hurry the shot. On defense, they will assume the role of whirling dervishes, and consume the spirit of your opponents and deny them the will to fight.

CHAPTER 4

---◼---

Can we do this?

You can do it. And that's not just a line from the Adam Sandler movie collection, either. You CAN DO it! Even if you are brand new to coaching basketball, this **Mongoose System** will walk you through this process step by step. We will be providing you with the offensive and defensive schemes and the practice objectives and drills you can use to teach your team the nuts and bolts, gradually feeding more and more complexities, when he team is ready. In fact, we think it may be more difficult to adapt to it if you have coached a long time and aren't open to new ideas. More than likely, you have coached some and even use some of these run and gun concepts, but have NOT committed nor considered committing to a basketball philosophy this innovative, and one some would consider radical. Again, let me assure you this "game plan" is not radical as it is not merely a game plan. It is a philosophy of play that begins at your first practice and continues on a journey until the final horn of your final game. For, it is in the practices that this philosophy is geminated and cultivated until it is harvested at the games.

Football coach Vince Lombardi famously ran a very simple offense which focused on execution. It is in the intricacies of the simple offense that the focus on this execution leads to mastery of it and, with this mastery, victory. Lombardi simplicity is the genius of using the **System** at the middle school level. It is not placing too much stress on your players by only beginning to teach the next higher program after they have mastered the previous one. Thus, confidence in their knowledge and execution will feed their <u>own</u> hunger to learn more, and have more fun with the **Mongoose System.** The three programs you teach are Mercury, Gemini and Apollo. Yes, we are all children of the space exploration era. We use President Kennedy's Rice University speech to inspire our teams and message that we do things in life, not because they are easy, but because they are hard. *Quia Difficilia Sunt.* <u>It is in the achievement of difficult things that we measure ourselves and others</u>. As President Kennedy cleverly put it to the crowd in terms of Texan college football reality, "why does Rice play Texas?"

Mercury

Mercury is where you build your team from the ground up and prepare them to launch, to break free of their earthen chains. In Mercury, your team can be successful and competitive on the court even without moving to the next program. The game systems to master in Mercury are:

- **Mongoose System** primary Break
- Pass for a shot
- Catch, Pivot & Shoot
- Shooting form
- Cross step and drive from spot
- Rotation of as many players as possible, as soon as the 1st quarter
- UCLA press defense
- Tech press defense

- "V" trapping
- Mongoose half court offense
- Maltese Cross half court defense
- Toy Soldier out of bounds play
- Picket Fence out of bounds play (under basket and side court)
- LMU Press Break

Once these concepts are mastered, then you can move on to teach additional concepts in the Gemini program.

Gemini

Gemini stacks concepts from Mercury and provides the additional framework to allow your team to maintain a successful orbit around other teams in your league, and will provide additional weapons for your team both offensively and defensively. In Gemini, your team will learn the following additional concepts:

- **Mongoose System** secondary break
- Full rotation of 5 players every minute (when local rules allow)
- Alcindor set play
- Two or more players become proficient at more than one position in **System**
- Puff press break
- Blitz full court press
- Box & 1 half court defense
- St. Peter out of bounds play
- Mercy out of bounds play
- Gideon side court play
- Tracking of **System** shooting objectives during the game

The ultimate program for our philosophy is Apollo. With the mastering of Apollo, your team will be in a position to go to the moon in your league. In it, the additional concepts you will incorporate are the following:

- Specialized player rotations (i.e. press group, rebound group, delay group)
- All or most players able to play at two or more positions in the **System**
- 4 corners delay offense
- Jailbreak press break
- Hickory out of bounds play
- Lion King out of bounds play
- Yellow Submarine side court play
- Pelican full court press
- Inclusion of at least 2 other half court set plays of your choosing
- Full Interval Conditioning Regimen
- Tracking of all 5 **System** statistics during the game
- The players themselves learn the Wooden Pyramid of Success

We will be going over, in depth, these programs and the concepts within each program in later chapters.

The more you coach, unless you are an unrefined and unrestrained narcissist, the more you realize that there is always more to learn and to pass on to others. You must have a healthy sense of narcissism in order to lead effectively and maintain your self-esteem and not be overly vulnerable to the slings and arrows that inherently are flung at you, the coach, but you must be able to keep it in check. One way to "check yourself" is to learn more about the art of coaching. If you have not taken any classes on how to coach there are excellent online classes offered by the

National Federation of State High School Association which also provide you with the opportunity for an accreditation as an interscholastic coach. We highly recommend these courses and the AAU also provides training in coaching through the Positive Coaching Alliance which is also an excellent and shorter online coaching class.

If you have not coached previously, or not taken any classes on how to coach, basic lessons are there to be learned that need to be second nature at the middle school level. Examples include.

- Learning to avoid profanity with children, especially in times of crisis and using other interjections to release tension. I know that as a young teen I was confused b my coaches repeated use of the phrase "geez Louise." I get it now. Using "oh bother" gets chuckles or rolled eyes from my players and other coaches, but it's one way of releasing frustration without being inappropriate.

- Understanding your job as coach is to have each player reach and surpass what THEY think is their potential. No A student can get a C and their parents expect that of you just as they push them as students to get achieve the best academically.

- You must learn to sandwich criticism of young players. That is, find a positive, take a coaching moment to criticize or teach, and then finish with a positive that hopefully shows the player how they will improve if they can learn from the lesson. The training from the AAU classes on coaching suggests the magic formula of 5:1, that is, try and give five positives for each criticism.

- You must treat all the players the equally, but not the same. Confused? Well, the best way to put it is to carefully evaluate each players' base skill level and then do your best to help each player improve along their own individual path not holding anyone back from development, actually pushing those with more talent harder than the others and not letting them settle by being the "best on the team." They must try and be the best they can be, period. This is because the specially gifted ones must understand the horizon isn't just the team, or best on the court, or the best at his or her age group. When you are fortunate to coach a young person who is clearly gifted, you must openly communicate with their parents and let them know you won't be allowing the child to settle in order to avoid potential misunderstandings about being picked on by the child.

Finally, how many chiefs, how many Indians? We have found it a successful coaching staff for the **Mongoose System** to have three coaches on the bench. Each coach can have a role that compliments your success. The head coach's role is tactical and moving forward and responsible for rotating players. The chief assistant's game time role is to track plus and minus plays that occur on the court and to discuss those with the group as they come off the court as the head coach cannot do this <u>and</u> push forward with the group newly on the floor. The second assistant, if you are able to get one, is responsible for tracking your shot chart which is the base metric for the Mercury-Apollo performance and can assist with coachable moments at all time stoppages.

The traditional scorekeeping task should be done by someone off the bench, and preferably a detail-oriented and attentive parent. You will want these later as these are individualized, BUT not as important to the team objectives in the course of the game. Later, in the Apollo program, you will need another person to keep track of offensive rebounds and turnovers caused by your players. This will require greater commitment from your parents, a team manager or assistant in order to keep these additional statistics, which again, are helpful in "day after' discussions with your team as to their overall performance.

As head coach, you won't be able to be the players' friend. If that's the role you are looking for, don't ask to be head coach because you won't be happy and you won't command the children's respect. We have found the delegation of player confidant, especially with girls, is best served by the second assistant coach whose role in the games is less game play coaching and more record keeper and bench cheerleader. Not that this coach is weak in any way, but she or he will be seen by the players as more approachable than the other two coaches, and we have found it best to openly communicate this coach's role to both the players and the parents.

Finally, we strongly recommend, even if you are a female head coach, have another female take on the role of second assistant on your team, especially with a girls team, as the incredible supportive and nurturing asset she can provide to the girls at this critical time of their growth and maturity (with its accompanying drama) cannot be understated. It also will make your job as head coach easier and more focused if your second assistant coach also acts as your general manager and responsible for logistics. Don't micromanage all the details that come with running a team, learn to delegate or have your second assistant delegate to responsible parents to perform tasks that free you up to run practices without distraction which will in turn maximize your time with your team.

CHAPTER 5

— ■ —

Parental controls

It's a great challenge to coach, and an even greater one to include some of your players' parents as your assistant coaches. As coaches, they will have complete access to their own child, and can provide an emotionally supportive role or sink your entire season by emotionally crippling your team by disruption. Which will it be? One cannot tell and it is always a calculated risk and your role, and theirs, must be clearly defined at the outset of the season and prior to the first practice, whenever possible. We see many middle school head coaches who do not and will not include parents as assistant coaches due to this potential pitfall.

If you are willing to take on the risk of a parental assistant, make sure to establish healthy boundaries for, he or she, when it comes to their own child and limit them from directly coaching them, whenever possible. Remember, there is no filter between a parent and their child and this "distance" will help maintain a healthy, though artificial, filter between them and your assistant can focus on other tasks you assign to them.

The **Mongoose System** to be most effective needs scorekeepers. One person to keep the regular scorebook, one to keep track of the shots on a shot chart, and another to track offensive rebounds and turnovers forced. As scorekeepers, parents can have an effective and extremely productive contribution to your team's success. The goals we are trying to achieve can thus be tracked and all your players can be made to more clearly to understand their part in the overall mission, even when their primary role in a game did not involve scoring.

Parents are invaluable volunteers to assist in morale and team building exercises throughout the season. They can be mobilized to perform all sorts of duties from handling concessions, taking tickets at the gym entrance to fund-raising. However, the greatest role they can play for team chemistry is to be supportive of the team mission and philosophy especially in the face of adversity. The **System** itself is not without its limitations and is not perfect. If it were, everyone would be using it, and even with flawless execution, sometimes shots will not fall. For example, we went an entire season being very successful, but one game we missed on all 26 3-pointers and lost in the semi-finals of the City Championship 23-18. Missing every 3-pointer had never happened to our team, but it did that day and even though we played outstanding defense, it wasn't to be out day.

This game style does create cardiac issues for some parents and family members because of the high octane intensity it carries with it. However, it will be highly detrimental if parents back away from supporting this philosophy, especially in front of their child, once a commitment is made to it. As the synoptic "gospel writers" of the **System** all agree, there is no halfway with it. It requires total immersion and if a player is pulled out of Portugal in the middle of the journey, she or he will never really be able to communicate in "Portuguese" language! Your players need to not only speak this language, but think in the language and embrace the culture of the **Mongoose System** in order to have the best opportunity to succeed with it. It's not jumping out of a plane without a parachute, but it may feel that way to some of your parents until they are converted along the road to Damascus.

This is different as the **Mongoose System** does not have starters. It has a "finishing" five. No starters is not what many people are accustomed to in sports and you must explain that a regular rotation can mean you are keeping everyone fresh and need your best five on the floor at the end of the half and, in particular, at the end of the game. You must walk through the philosophy with your parents and how your mission is to improve each player's fundamentals and maximize their athleticism through this style of play. Don't be negative with them, but the reality is that 90% of youth players do NOT play high school varsity basketball. They can learn so much from the lessons the game teaches – portable lessons they will carry with them the rest of their lives when combined with the belief they were an important part of a real team.

CHAPTER 6

■

Player buy-in to the Mongoose System

Although to some of the fathers of the **System** it may sound heretical or extreme, we believe our **Mongoose System,** which is based upon a combination of the LMU, Grinnell, Redlands, and Olivet Nazarene Systems, <u>is</u> not merely possible for use at the middle school and youth levels, but the ideal. You also have the opportunity coaching it at this level in not having your players "unlearn" other types of philosophies when you introduce it to them.

The first player point is that everyone has a role and that each role is responsible to every other role on the team. We are an interwoven piece of chain armor surrounding the heart of our team. Any chink in this armor will open our heart to mortal danger.

Next, everyone has value to our team. Some players are shooters, some rebound well, some are speedy and some are outstanding defensive players. Regardless of their raw athleticism, each player can and will contribute to the wellness of the body. Your job as coach is to put each player in the position to best provide that value to the team and that player's confidence will go up and so will their production.

Explain to the team early, the **Mongoose System** philosophy can find its roots in the campaigns of Napoleon. We always start by telling them Napoleon was a general who lived "once upon a time, in a galaxy far, far away." Napoleonic battlefield tactics had four distinct characteristics.

First, artillery was used to break up the enemy defenses and disorient their morale. It didn't matter that the artillery did not actually kill many men with one shot, it was the sound and explosive impact it made when it did hit that caused fear and anxiety on their opponents. Likewise, our artillery is the use of the 3 point shot. They don't all have to hit, heck we'd be happy if a third of them hit! But, its force casts a heavy blow to the morale of the opponent and disrupts their tight zone defense at this level.

Second, infantry was used to drive forward, with the naked bayonet, with force of will and courage to dislodge the enemy from its fixed position which had just been rocked by the artillery. It was for the infantry to finish the job. For us, it is in the offensive rebounding and second and third shots under the glass to finish the job for us. Without effective rebounding, all the artillery in the world won't bring us to victory!

Third, cavalry was the tool that crowned the victory by taken the scattered foe and riding them into the dirt. Horses running down shattered and isolated opponents with sabers flashing against the sun would utterly devastate the enemy. In the **Mongoose System,** our cavalry is our press defense. When we complete the mission on our trip down the court by scoring with artillery or infantry, our opponents are disoriented. It is then that the cavalry is most effective by swirling and trapping, and then diving into the passing lanes to steal the ball and capitalize on the damaged morale of the other team. It is here they will be broken and where not merely a run can begin, but we can cut a huge swath through their lines from which they may be unable to recover!

Finally, Napoleonic battles were largely battles of intense close quarter attrition with limited true opportunities for maneuver. They required high morale to maintain troops throughout the ordeal. Napoleon famously kept his best troops in reserve, his Imperial Guard, and only committed them when both sides were near exhaustion, to carry the day with these fresh and most devastating troopers. The **Mongoose System** is set up to keep all your players in rotation and rested so that at the end of the battle, you will be able to place your "Imperial Guard," your Finishing 5, onto the floor with energy and devastating power against your opponent whose team will then be drained and on its heels. As Coach Lombardi said, "fatigue makes cowards of us all." It is in this fatigue your enemy is suffering from that your Finishing 5 will be able to take advantage and dominate.

A direct way to express need to rotate players on the team is to have the five fastest players dribble the ball five times up and down the court and have the others in groups of five run as a relay team one time down the court. It will show to them how tired a player will get if he or she has no relief. To drive the point home, you then repeat it and watch their reaction. We have been fortunate that all we have had to say is, O.K., let's go again, and the "fastest" kids have gotten the lesson without having to repeat it!

It can be easy for the primary shooters to be excited about the opportunity to be gunners think themselves middle school folk heroes by launching from downtown, but the real money shots are from the 3, 4 & 5 who clean up the table with rebounds and second chances. They also are taking much higher percentage field goal opportunities so they are able to score, sometimes higher totals, even though they take fewer shots. Again, use this as a coachable moment and explain to your players that this is their opportunity to show the value they bring to the team, under the boards. They, just like the late Hank Gathers at LMU, will clean up all the crumbs around the basket and be full by the time the game ends!

We keep multiple stats for strategic reasons, for goal setting too, but also for value added reasons. What I mean is that the **Mongoose System** is the perfect vehicle to track stats that will raise the confidence of all your players as every one of them can not only get a chance to shoot, but also to force turnovers, and rip down offensive rebounds. We routinely ask the players at half time and the end of the game to raise their hands if they shot the ball. It is the chance for success, it is in the quest to reach competitive greatness that we track and it shows returns as the players begin to strive each day to get higher up that mountain!

Tell your players the story of Rikki Tikki Tavi. Rikki was a mongoose kept by an English family in India who had to bite the necks of two deadly cobras and kill them in order to save the lives of that family. A mongoose is incredibly quick and agile and able to go toe to toe with the cobra. The 4 on our team must be that mongoose in our defensive schemes even though he or she may be the shortest or least athletic on the team in the beginning. The performance of the 4 will make or break your defensive strategy and must be groomed to play within their abilities and then, step by step, elevated to his or her true potential. And this potential may not even be seen by the player, until driven to achieve it. We have found that even though a player may begin as the 4, they may develop and blossom and be able play additional positions which will give you more weaponry.

Another chance to explain the value of team and each individual's contribution to the body is the story of Stone Soup. This story is from a long time ago (and a galaxy far far away) and it about a stranger coming into a country village, hungry and looking for food. He knocks on several doors, but no one gives him any food. The village has a central large cauldron, or pot, in the center of it. The stranger goes to the well and fills it with water, grabs some wood, and proceeds to build a fire under the cauldron. The villagers are watching the stranger now with confusion and yet also curiosity. They watch next as the stranger begins looking around the center square and stops to closely inspect several large stones of different shape. The stranger has five stones set before him on the table next to the now heated water in the cauldron. At this point, one of the braver villagers comes outside and questions the stranger as to what in the world he was doing. The stranger tells the villager he is about to make stone soup, the best soup east of the Pecos. The villager is interested and wants to try it when he is done cooking it. The stranger tells him that, of course, he can have some and that the one other thing that would make it perfect is if there was any salt lying around to slightly season the stones. The villager eagerly responded he had some salt and went and got it. Well, this was repeated again and again with celery, onions, and eventually a chicken thrown in by other inquisitive villagers. Your team needs to dig down and bring what they have in their own personal supply of goods and bring it to your team's mission. With everyone's contribution, even though we may start with only a stone at first, when all contribute to the body, we will most certainly feast in the end.

We suggest your team and their parents with you watch the Guru of Go film which has about a 45 minute running time. It is a story of triumph and tragedy. It may be too much for elementary level players, but we have found it to include the how, what and why of the **System** and in an intensely dramatic manner. It was the genesis of why we began to coach this way, and it will open the door for your players to understand why they run and what the rewards can be. It does not explain the rotational part of what we do, and this can be explained to them as stated above. As we will discuss in Chapter 9, the rotation we suggest was taught to us through lessons from Coach Arseneault in his writings, video, and practical application of it at Grinnell College.

When your players give their all to the mission of the team, they will be all invested in its results. Coach Lombardi said, "The harder you work, the harder it is to surrender." This is because of that personal commitment a player makes to excellence will internally drive them in the final extremity to reach, obtain, and overcome even in the face of insurmountable obstacles. Thus, we must teach our players that the greatest effort and preparation = boundless confidence in themselves and their teammates.

Most importantly, your players must be told again and again that the **Mongoose System** is designed not to hold anyone back, not to take away playing time, but instead to unleash their potential greatness. They will shoot more. They will be more active! They will perform without boundaries on their capability! It is up to them to decide, as players, how high they will reach for the next step up that mountain.

Player buy-in most readily occurs, in our experience, through their becoming a family. This is done through team building and because it is so important to the **Mongoose System** and its success, we have broken out a whole chapter about it. It's coming up next!

CHAPTER 7

■

Utilizing Team Building
and Life Lessons

I saw this important coaching lesson on NFL Films "Harbaugh Family Roundtable" film, "teach them a fact and they'll learn, tell them the truth and they'll believe, but tell them a story and they will remember it for the rest of their lives." Life lessons have been taught through the medium of storytelling since the caveman. We use these time tested stories to instruct and team building.

The core of these progressive life lessons we teach comes straight from Coach Wooden's Pyramid of Success. We have incorporated his lessons into how we teach at practices and attempt to have our players focus on them as we progress through our pre-season practice objectives. For one of our teams, we have even purchased copies of **Coach Wooden's Pyramid of Success: Building Blocks for a Better Life** and had each of them read it and memorize the pyramid before they could receive their practice jerseys that had their name on the back! This was an Apollo program team who already had heard over and over these lessons and we wanted to encourage further learning about their final game season together. This book is must reading for all coaches.

We begin each season; no matter if it is 5th grade youth at the YMCA or 8th grade middle school ball with the Bible story of David & Goliath. We have one or more of the players read it out loud in front of the team and then discuss the lesson. It teaches walking into a valley to face a terrible foe that others were afraid to confront. It teaches that you can overcome your greatest challenge through faith and focus in the task before you.

As we mentioned earlier, the **Guru of Go** video provides a colorful and dramatic telling in story form of how the **System** works, but it tells so much more. It tells of team, of commitment, of loyalty to a style of play after the players bought into it that will convey to your own players a message of what they themselves are capable of, if they believe. We show it every season in school ball to our new set of parents and players right after the first couple of practices to educate them on how this can work and how much fun we can have. The DVD extras also have interviews that further explain these concepts and how the **System** itself is a successful offense. Again, this is a mandatory teaching tool for the **Mongoose System** to be understood and for team building to begin.

We show the movie **Miracle** to our players for team building, and this has been shown the night before a big tournament to them. One, it has a great message and reinforces what we been teaching them and, two, we tell them to go to sleep on time after this team meeting and KNOW where they were the night before the big event begins! A big deal when it comes to boys and girls in 8th grade! **Miracle** not only illustrates that anything is possible in a tournament, even defeating the greatest team in the world, immediately after the beat your team like a drum the week before, but several other key ideas. One, the rotation of a hockey team is <u>exactly</u> what we are doing on a basketball court. We have two lines that rotate in turn, and sometimes rotate a few more players into the game on the "third" line. This helps prove the point to your players that after sprinting for a minute or two, teams rotate their players on the ice/court. Next, it shows how a team of "All-stars" must decide, must choose, to come together if they want to win and become a family. In the movie, this is graphically shown as former national championship rivals must fight each other and eventually reconcile to complete the mission the team is driven to finish. In our experience, some of the middle school drama that is generated by them and swirling around them can seem larger to our players than the Olympics in the middle of the Cold War!

Just as football teams have their pride stickers on helmets, we have found great value in team victory stripes on hair ribbons for our girls' teams. They have their name on the ribbon and their number and on the other side of the ribbon for their pony tail are basketball stickers that run down the other side of the ribbon. They wore them in the game as part of their uniform and at school to promote their team spirit. Players' parents also invested in shooter shirts and reversible practice jerseys which we helped organize through team discount purchases. These also helped to establish an *espirit d' corps* and unit loyalty for our team. Both of these items were purchased with our players' names on the back of them and our team on the front with the phrase "organized chaos" under a basketball.

We use music, our music, which is sanitized to keep some of the drills moving and add noise to the practices, especially when they are doing 5 on 0 drills and shooting exercises. Make sure to pause it when you are trying to make a point, or they may still be humming the theme from **Rocky** and not focusing on the point you are trying to make.

And when I say the players' names, I mean their nicknames. Each player is assigned a nickname, no exceptions, even if it a simple derivation of their formal name. Nicknames that are unique to the team help to establish the separate team identity needed to fuel the **Mongoose System**. They must leave their other world behind them when they enter the gym. Our players, at a catholic middle school, are told that al practice, they can only discuss three things, Jesus, Mary, or basketball. All other subjects are *verboten*, forbidden!

We pick two permanent team captains whose responsibilities are to be team leaders. They are to promote team harmony and build morale. This means game time and class time and does not stop when the team leaves the gym. At this age level, it's best not to allow the players to vote on these positions. It is an important lesson in responsibility for your players in naming them captains, but should not be applied until the Gemini program. At Apollo, we suggest naming another player as the game captain and rotate that assignment as all players need to step up with leadership at this point in your program.

We use a pre-tip cheer before we hit the court. It allows the team to start the game in a moment of unity and power. We really liked the "draw blood" line from the movie **Heart of the Game** so we included in the end of our cheer and even the girls liked it! For the girls:

Pretty, power, smart
Mongoose, Rikki, Tikki, Tavi,
Eagles (insert your team nickname),
Bite the cobra (said just by game captain), draw blood (rest of team),

Bite the cobra (said just by game captain), draw blood (rest of team),

Bite the cobra (said just by game captain), draw blood (rest of team).

For the boys, it's the same except the first three words are replaced with:

Hustle, power, smart.

Finally, we insist on doing simple trust exercises to bring our players together, reinforce the refrain from **Semi-Pro** that "everybody loves everybody," and even have the team split and play dodge ball against each other at the end of practice during the season. Dodge ball is not just a fun game, but it reinforces agility training, catching, full-court vision, and most of all the killer instinct.

CHAPTER 8

■

Who do you keep and cut?

If you are just starting out with a fresh group of young people, our advice is to not cut anyone. Even when there is a mandatory play requirement in your league keep everyone because your primary goal as coach and teacher is to help each player improve and provide the life lessons basketball can imbue to them. You just don't know who will grow the following year. You can't predict whose awkwardness will develop her or him into a finely honed agile cat. You shouldn't judge that a nine year old's current level of immaturity, especially upon first glance at a try out, is incorrigible.

Unless your team has progressed to the Apollo program, don't cut ANYONE who can provide value. Even when your middle school or youth league has mandatory play requirements, you can use the additional players, up to a full dozen players. If your league does not require mandatory play, then you want as many players as possible and this number now runs to fifteen. You may not be able to immediately integrate all the players into your rotation, but these extra players will be valuable to build your team and if you could work with them enough to have three separate lines in a rotation, it will exponentially increase the reserve value of your Finishing 5. It will make practices more fruitful and in games your pressure defense will spark with greater electricity.

One rule to remember, don't keep players who DON'T want to be there. There will be some kids who come out for tryouts, but don't want to be there and are only there because their parents wanted them to tryout. You must attempt to find out in the tryout process if they truly want to be there and are willing to dedicate themselves to the mission. This is critical as if they are on your team and your team runs the **Mongoose System**, you are committing to play that person in a rotation which also means you are taking minutes away from another child. Further, if your league has a mandatory play rule, and most do at middle school and youth leagues these days, then you will be hurting your entire team by playing that person. As a coach, you can inspire, and you are supposed to light the pilot light on your players' heater, but you don't want to have to walk down the stairs into the basement try and find it, in the dark.

No one likes cutting people from a team. Unfortunately, you may have more than the number of people you are willing to keep on your team or your AD wants you to limit your team to ten players. If this is the case, and you are compelled to cut players, for the **Mongoose System** to have its best opportunity for success, we recommend you should be looking for speed first, then stamina, then height. Always take the gutsiest players over those will not withstand the trials and tribulations this philosophy will bring, especially when your team has a bad run during a game. Those moments happen and you aren't needing any players who use the worst four letter word ever - **can't**.

CHAPTER 9

■

Player Rotations

The **Mongoose System** will be your strongest weapon for maintaining a happy home life if you are a parent trying to coach your own child. This is because fundamentally it treats all players fairly with approximately the same playing time which is the base question all youth players and their parents ask of a coach. Is my child playing a fair amount of time? How many times did we used to hear it when we first started coaching youth sports some twenty (20) years ago? The **Mongoose System** solves that potential problem, but it gives you the next set of problems as to playing time and that is, how come my child isn't playing enough?

We rotate the maximum number of players we can, every minute of play, and play in leagues with 6 minute quarters, stopped time. Players get up from the bench and go to the scorer's table at the 45 second mark on the clock and then enter the game at the next stoppage mark. Sometimes, each line gets a little above or below the minute shift, but it balances out. When we have rules that require players to play a full one quarter without being subbed out, we get these mandatory full quarters out of the way as soon as possible and then execute the full rotation in the second half.

We don't have true "starters." We tell all the players this as well and there is great value to making sure you have your stronger line, or least your more effective speed line in at the end of the quarters when your opponents are worn out and more vulnerable to your pressure defense and transition.

We have finishers. We come out of our regular rotation the final two minutes of every game and bring in our Finishing 5. This is our Imperial Guard, as previously stated, and due to our rotation these five players are better fit for the final kick to the end the race. This requires you to select how you want to finish and the personnel required to achieve that goal. After greater sophistication in the **System,** you will be able to sub in individual players from your bench on offense and defense when needed in to your Finishing 5. We won critical games by use of our team's flexibility in subbing in a trapper on the defensive end and then subbing her out and replacing her with a 3-point shooter when we resumed control of the ball.

The forming of Special Situation 5 groups, like Rebounding 5, Delay 5, or Trapping 5, is not something that is really possible until you reach the Gemini or Apollo programs. You can do it sooner in their development, but best to wait. You can form a Shooting 5 as easily as a Finishing 5 in Mercury though.

You must practice these rotational switches over and over and write out your rotational shifts before the first game, and be prepared to alter it if the chemistry of the shifts needs "refreshing." We have included a couple rotational charts in the Appendix. One rotation listed in the Appendix is for twelve players with no mandatory "full quarter" play required, and one is for eight players where each player must play a full uninterrupted quarter by local league rule.

CHAPTER 10

——————— ■ ———————

Teaching Basketball Fundamentals

The greatest misconception about the **System** when I talk to other coaches who have not coached it or parents who are not used to seeing it executed is the belief it is a gimmick and does not teach fundamental basketball skills. However, other middle school coaches and youth coaches who do understand it have been highly complementary of the improvement it has brought out in our teams and parents we have coached have almost universally testified as to the enormous improvement it has brought out in their own child's ability. Use of our **Mongoose System** at the middle school and youth levels goes to the heart of making players more fundamentally sound in the following areas:

Shooting

We have had referees during breaks in games come up to us and tell us they have never seen teams shoot so effectively at this level of play. And we aren't shooting at a much higher field goal percentage than other teams, but we are shooting more, and at least as good a FG percentage! So, it appears we shoot "better" because we are scoring more, and at times, in bunches. And there are hot streaks in shooting, everyone knows that and when those moments happen, it does look magical.

This magic is born in the sweat and repetition of practice time. Of shooting over and over again from the spots the players anticipate shooting in the game. It is focusing on teaching proper shooting form. Starting with the shooting flip and finishing with their "hand in the cookie jar" we constantly check the players to perform with the proper technique.

Shooting accuracy is strengthened by this repetitive drilling. We have the boys and girls form a semi-circle around the goal and work on shooting flip. We move them to shoot from the blocks and use the board. We have them run and shoot from their "spots" in the **Mongoose System** in both the primary and secondary breaks when time for offensive technical drills are scheduled during practice. We then pull these out of our bag whenever we want to reinforce these skills and also when they are *run out* and need to have a pause from a running drill. It also helps them to focus on shooting when they are a bit fatigued, which is what happens in the game itself.

Layup form is practiced one step at a time for all players. Layups are routinely polished for our players in the offensive technical drills section of practice. We like to combine lay ups with shooting from their spots by doing our own version of the full court layup drill. We line up in the middle of the court all players capable of playing the 1, and the rest of the players line up along the sideline beginning at half court. The first 1 takes the ball and dribbles twice from our defensive free throw line and then throws the ball to a player who has already broken to his or her "spot." From this spot, the player receives the ball, pivots towards the basket and fires away. After this initial shot, either a miss or make, the player runs the ball down and throws it in from out of bounds to the 1 who then races back down the court to perform a full court layup. The other player trails, rebounds the layup, and then throws it to the next 1 in line who then repeats the exercise. We use two balls beginning the second ball after the first shot is taken. There is more attention to layups when we begin polishing offensive and defensive skills as the season progresses.

Dribbling

In the **Mongoose System,** there is clearly the recognition that most middle school and youth teams are not chocker-block full of boys and girls who have 5 star dribbling skills when we get them. We are first and foremost trying to move quickly and still minimizing our own turnovers. We do this by having our players get the ball into the hands of our 1 as soon as can when our opponent makes a basket. On a missed basket, we then outlet to our 1 as soon as we can and he or she drives the court at full speed. That being said, we focus on dribbling drills for all players from day one to increase each players' proficiency, obviously with emphasis on the 1.

Passing & receiving passes

Players work on passing form and speed each practice. They work swinging passes to open teammates and quickly to set up scoring opportunities. Players are taught to "pass for a shot," as Coach Westhead put it, and always use the pass as an attacking weapon. The pass is taught to be made on target to enable their teammate to then use the ball without delay for a shot. The art of catching a ball properly cannot be understated at this level. As the team moves quickly, they are prone to lose focus and make mistakes. You must teach your team to catch the ball with their dominant hand with a stop sign target and use their other hand to pull the ball into them. Catching in this manner allows them to immediately be positioned to then unload a shot.

Rebounding

Critical to the success of the **Mongoose System** is rebounding. On both boards, our players must pull down the rock and finish. On offense, they must be able to track our shots, anticipate the angle of deflection on a missed shot, and then attack and retrieve. The next shot is always the most important shot and it must be ours! On defense, finding the ball and attacking the boards to deny our opponents additional shots, especially if they have broken our press, is essential. We teach our players on defense to not delay getting the outlet to our 1 once we have the ball and begin the transition.

Pick & Roll

We teach proper screening techniques to our players beginning with our 5 and 4 positions that learn this when we teach the "whole" of the primary break of the **Mongoose System**. Learning how to come off a screen is just as important as the setting of the screen and this technique is taught and re-taught. The 1, 2 & 3 players all must learn this in order to be effective in the offense and we teach our players to come off the screen, off-ball, with their hands up looking for the ball immediately. We drill this skill which is then portable for our players with any offense they move on to with other teams.

Basketball IQ

In the **Mongoose System,** players are taught to attack the basket whenever they can. Most players at this level must be empowered to believe they are capable of great things on the court. The ability to attack the rim without hesitation is a skill they must learn if they want to succeed at any level. It is a skill that can then be polished and expanded upon through the progression of programs from Mercury to Apollo. Players learn to shoot, drive or pass for another player to assault the basket. This is the point of this philosophy, to attack on both offense and defense. It is to be constantly tuned in when you are on the court and if you don't have the ball, you must be actively ready to move for the ball or open up your teammate to make him or her an offensive threat. So, in any offense they will play later, their next coach will be able to teach them their scheme and the player will already have a base understanding of always being an active participant on the floor.

Defensive stance & footwork

We teach defensive footwork to our players to enable them to effectively pressure the ball everywhere on the court. Teaching your players at this level the discipline to work with proper footwork on defense will enable them to better pressure your opponents and provide the lynchpin to both your full court and half court games. The proper defensive stance whey need to use is not natural for these boys and girls and it is only through repetition that you will enable them to perform during the game with the correct balance and ability to disrupt your opponents to the best of their ability.

Trapping & intercepting the ball

On-ball trapping is a chief skill taught to our players in the **Mongoose System**. Players must be able to work together to funnel a ball handler into the vortex of the trap and then collapse on the ball. They must be able to prevent the ball handler from driving outside of the trap and then breaking the entire press in the back court. Trapping in the half court defense involves every player on our team except for our 5, and so almost all of our players learn this skill. If players aren't trapping on defense, they are Interceptors. They are looking to steal a pass at all times. This means aggressively covering the "near man" to the ball handler and not merely covering thin air. Only by covering the closest players to the ball will full pressure be applied to your opponents. Our players learn to shift into the passing lanes and anticipate the next threatening pass of our opponents and try and beat them to the pass. When trappers and interceptors work in concert, it looks like a dance. As Coach Wooden puts it, the press requires all players to be working together as one, and it is the ultimate expression of team and synchronized movement on the court.

Free Throws

We practice free throws regularly after we build our foundation and bricks on our home. Players shoot free throws better when they have the confidence to shoot them. We work with them to use the proper technique, minimizing their body movements when they shoot, to minimize error rate. When you shoot this often, you will draw fouls especially when your opponents get tired as they will lose focus and hopefully their mental edge along with it. This then, will result in your team creating foul shot opportunities and must be practiced regularly to take advantage of these situations. We often tell our teams that the only way our opponents can slow us down is to foul us so be happy when they foul us because that's an indication they are in trouble. One team, in an 8th grade middle school game we played, fouled out four of its players in the first half!

Polish later in the season

All players' skills will be polished as your team progresses through the season's practices. As coach and teacher, you decide based on your resources and coaching staff how many sub-groups you will be able to have to instruct on these technical skills. It is our opinion with the **Mongoose System**, you must begin by teaching the whole so the players will understand the "whys" of these technical skills and this will enable them to better appreciate the "hows" of them when explained to them. You will also decide how much time during the in-season practices to focus your limited time on specific aspects of these technical skills. The **Mongoose System** does recommend you spend your time, as we do, 2:1 on offensive skills to defensive technical skills.

CHAPTER 11

■

Drill, Drill & drill...
Practicing effectively

As coach, practices are where the **Mongoose System** is made. It is through constant moving and deliberative drilling, over and over again, that your players will find the confidence in themselves and each other for success. In this journey, you are building a home for your team family to live in. In order for that home to withstand the icy winds of winter, that home must be built with a solid foundation, walled with the finest Old Chicago bricks, reinforced with mortar by a skilled craftsman, and finished with a Spanish Tile roof. Only after this home is built through the grit and sweat of these practices can your team ascend the mountain top of competitive greatness as described by Coach Wooden. The point when your team plays its best, when its' best is required!

We have broken our practice regimen into "weeks." You should augment this "weekly" schedule into five parts, depending on how much time you have going into your first week of play. This schedule is designed to be finished running into your first week of game play. We suggest you decide which programmatic level of difficulty you choose to work your team at and then utilize the following practice schedule in which to teach it.

Week 1 - Foundation

- Learn the **Mongoose System**
- Out of bounds plays
- Technical drills – Offense
  - *Dribbling*
  - *Cross-over penetration move*
  - *Passing*
  - *Shooting*
  - *Rebounding*
- Half court defense - introduction

Week 2 - Bricks

- Learn Full Court Defense
- Learn Half Court Defense
- Technical Drills – Defense
  - *Defensive stance*
  - *Defensive slide*
  - *"V" trapping*
  - *Off-ball interceptor position & response*
- Review the **Mongoose System**
- Review out of bounds plays
- Shooting drills

Week 3 - Mortar

- Review & add second - Full Court defense
- Review & add second – Half Court defense
- Review the **Mongoose System**
  - *Pick & Roll drill*

- UCLA 3 on 2 drill
- Full Court layups
- Rebound and outlet drill
- Introduce Press break(s)
- 3 on 5 Press drill
- 3 on 5 Press Break drills

Week 4 - Spanish Tile Roof

- Technical Precision & Confidence Drills
  - *Pivoting out of trouble*
  - *Shooting flip*
  - *3 pointers (sets of 10)*
  - *5 & 4 passes and shots*
  - *Defensive spacing*
  - *Drop step on defense*
  - *Denial on defense*
  - *Free throws (shots and response)*
- **Mongoose System**
  - *Rotation practice*
  - *"Full game" drills*
- Review out of bounds plays
- Set Play incorporation
- Introduce Delay Offense

Week 5 - The Mountain Top

- Review the **Mongoose System** Offense
  - *Focus on transition from every situation*
  - *Shooting drills within* **System**
  - *"Full game" drills with rotations*
- Review Out of bounds plays
- Review set plays

- Review Full Court Press
  - *"V" trapping*
  - *3 on 5 drills*

***If you are choosing to work the Apollo program, we further suggest that your interval conditioning training (*See Chapter 12*) begin in week 1 and be strictly adhered to through week 4 of the schedule below which will extend your practice times by 30 minutes or you will be using it in place of other drills.

We think an ideal practice at this level for the **Mongoose System** should last no longer than 90 minutes. It is your responsibility as coach to keep the players constantly engaged during these practices. Lombardi said this well before we did in his book, **Run to Daylight**. During your regular season, if you are in a situation like us, gym time gets very tight for teams at this level as multiple teams use the gym and many nights are filled with games by these teams. Therefore, your practice time may even be more limited. We spend much of our seasonal practices in polishing fundamentals and reviewing our **Mongoose System** and our full court press and press break. Depending on the team we have in a particular season, those fundamentals we need to polish may shift and this will certainly be the case for you too. We have a suggested amount of time in a routine one-hour practice we believe to be the most beneficial for your team, and these times can be adjusted to add more time to them if you get the full 90 minutes. Specifically,

In-season one-hour practice focus

• **Mongoose System** offense	15 minutes
• Out of bounds plays	5 minutes
• Full court Press defense	10 minutes

- Offensive technical drills   10 minutes
- Defensive technical drills   5 minutes
- Scrimmage (using no press)   10 minutes
- Team building finish:
  - *"Put out" or dodge ball*   *5 minutes*

TOTAL = 60 MINUTES

One trick we have used to maximize court time is to have each ball player get his or her own water jug and bring it to practice and have it near them at all times so as to not lose time "walking" to the water fountains, standing in line, and then the usual visiting or gossiping. Another is to have our players meet thirty minutes prior to our assigned court time for conditioning, chalk talk, or introduction of new concepts. This allows for no wasted time on the court itself. Drills we routinely use are:

Team Offense

- 5 on zero
- 5 on 3
- 5 on zero for the whole game and keep score with your rotation (primary & secondary break
- 5 on 4 drill
- Practicing your Press breaks
- Scrimmaging against betters
- Full contact scrimmages with scoring kept...

Offensive Technical Drills

- Dribbling gauntlet
- Pivot & pass gauntlet
- Dodge a chair and dodge a ball dribbling
- Rebounding 5 on 3 drill

- Cross step and drive
- Full court lay up
- UCLA drill
- 3 point shooting from all 5 shooting locations drill
- Pivoting out of trouble on defensive rebound and outlet pass to 1

Team Defense

- Practicing the Press defense
- Scrimmaging against betters
- Full contact scrimmages with scoring kept...

Defensive Technical Drills

- "v" trapping
- Blitz – near man denial and trapping
- Defensive position and slide drill Defensive spacing for one on one – on ball
- Defensive spacing and denial - off ball
- 2 on 1 Safety drill

The "endgame" of your season needs to be one that works to avoid burn out by your players and helps them reach for the stars. We include more and more team building activities and assure ourselves that we minimize additional injuries at this time when we want to finish strongly. Also, it helps to heal both physically and mentally when players have been pushed and whipped so hard during the season. Some of your players will not have run this hard in their lives and not experienced such a pounding, but as we have said, we believe if the results come in, your players will learn a whole new side of themselves, and they will develop a pride that even their parents will have not yet seen.

CHAPTER 12

■

Conditioning and fitness

Your team must be running in practice all the time. If they are not running, they are resting and listening to you in front of the chalk board or doing drills which allow them to catch their breath, like a free throw drill. Move them from drill to drill and don't lose precious practice time and let them walk around burning daylight. You are "mentally" conditioning your team by this process to <u>never</u> be walking on the court. Every player shows his or her value by running and wearing their opponents down by this force of will.

Always running with the ball or off-ball must be programmed into your players' minds and when you are fortunate to have 10 or more players, you can rotate your players before they get fatigued and thereby lose intensity. Coach Arseneault states in his book and video presentations that players in the **System** cannot maintain intensity for more than a minute or two's time on the court. He further tells us that after this time, players will subconsciously hold back and "save" strength through the shift, at times.

We have found this to be true at the middle school and youth levels, but have had to accommodate our **Mongoose System**, at times, to meet local rules which require players to play a full uninterrupted quarter. This rule is designed to ensure all players on a team have some game time participation. Allowing player participation is not an issue for us and this rule only serves to handicap our team, however, we attempt to check off this requirement as early in the game as possible.

At the **Mongoose System** level of middle school and youth play, no player can afford to hold back and must play with reckless abandon. In many instances, the players themselves are learning the fine points of the game and are neophytes to even playing something other than school intramurals and if they hold back, they will lose confidence, and diminish their aggressiveness on the court, and your opponent will feed off these vulnerabilities.

With our team running often in drills throughout every practice, it may be a surprise to you that we run no suicides. That's right, no suicides. We run with the ball, we run 5 on zero drills, 5 on 3 drills, full court layup drills, and UCLA 3 on 2 drills, BUT NO SUICIDES. This is done intentionally to have them run the court and make it fun, make it functional and give them a prize for running. Instead of eh old miss a free throw and negatively say, now everybody, suicide, we tell them we are running to win. We try to make sprinting fun for them so they will buy into the program even more.

When you reach Apollo, we recommend you institute interval training for your team. The exercises we incorporate into ours are designed to challenge the players to do as many of the particular exercises in the two minute limit. This will train your team to maximize their effort in two minute intervals and push them through the following exercises:

- Dribbling the length of the court – back and forth
- Shot from their spot - made
- Push ups

- Layups - made
- Sit ups
- Free throws - made (5 minutes – not rushed)
- Burpies

We chose two minute intervals for these exercises to make it easier for them to drive themselves mentally and physically through the one minute they will work on the court. In order to make this work for you and your team with maximum results, you **must** create a workout sheet for each player with the exercises and space for them to place their results. Charting this progress is essential to their gaining in strength and confidence. We do this with Mercury and Gemini program teams only intermittently and when we are able to keep players for more than the regular 60 or 90 minute practice times.

When one player makes a mistake in practice, everybody runs a lap. We know there are counterarguments in the coaching training with the National Federation of High Schools about not using conditioning for discipline as players begin to equate it with negativity. However, when we begin practicing, we explain to the players they are all important and no one can simply nod off or lose focus.

Finally, a mistake by one player in basketball affects everyone as all are dependent upon each other for success. Helping to ingrain that philosophy is when one makes a mistake, all run a lap. We tell the team that the person who made the mistake must re-focus on not repeating the mistake and realize how he or she has impacted his or her teammates. Second, for the players who did not make the mistake, it is to be looked upon as an opportunity to be better fit and realize they also don't want to lose focus.

CHAPTER 13

■

Mongoose System - Primary Break

The **Mongoose System** works at the middle school and youth levels because it simplifies the game for your players and allows them to all learn quickly their roles and maximize their value by performing that role to the best of their ability. Just as Coach Lombardi had his signature play, the Green Bay Sweep, this is our signature play. Similarly, they both find their success in execution, poise and determination. How it works is simple and can be run against man or zone defenses at this level of play. It can be run when there is a made basket or a missed one.

First, when your opponents make a basket, your 5 player, who is the only person to throw the ball in on your end, goes and gets the ball and immediately throws it in play. If you are in a youth league that does not allow full court pressing on made baskets, we recommend you have your 4 player throw the ball in every time and allow your 5 player time to run into their position down the floor. We want to get the ball into the hands of the 1 as soon as possible in our regular made or missed basket break and allow that person to run the floor as our quarterback. The 1 is to take a dribble or two and pass the ball if a player is open. If not, take the ball and penetrate to the middle of the floor, staying a little to the right in the classic LMU version of the **System**. As Coach Westhead says, the 1 is "passing for a shot."

In the **Mongoose System**, the 1 drives down the center-right of the court looking to pass to an open teammate in this order of progression, every time, 3-2-5-4. If none of them are open, and he or she is not opposed the 1 is to drive for the basket. This will result in a basket or if challenged, then dish to the open player. If the 1 passes the ball to a teammate, she or he then stays high and does <u>not</u> rebound. The 1 is our defensive safety unless he or she drives all the way to the rim. If this happens, the 2 rotates to the top of the key and becomes the safety.

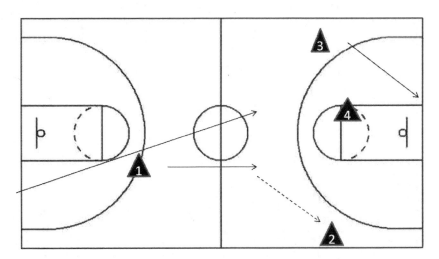

The 1 is first to look down the court to the 3. If the 3 is there and no defender is back in the paint, the 1 is to throw the ball ahead to the 3 who runs it down and finishes with a layup or jump stop from the left block under the basket. The 3 has run the floor on the left side and heads all the way to the left block always looking back for the ball, ready to receive it and finish.

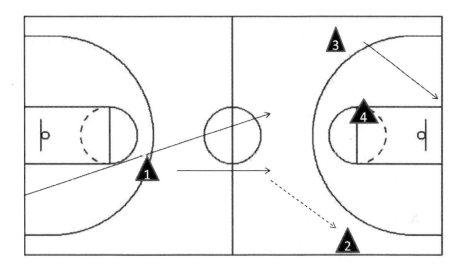

The next option is for the 1 to look to the 2 who sets up for a 3 point shot on the right wing. The 2 is to let it fly if open. If overplayed, the 2 is to cross step and drive to the hole. If correctly played by the defender, the 2 is to look first to the 4 who cuts to the near block, next to the 5 who has shifted to the left elbow (where the 4 started), and third, back to the 1 who is also perched at the 3 point line with proper spacing from the 2.

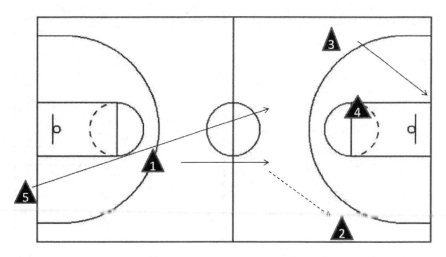

Next, the 2 must be court aware and if covered on the wing is to then cut around the court to the other wing after catching a pick from the 3 under the basket. The 1 uses a pick from the 5 on top and pushes the ball towards the 2. If the 1 is open, she or he may take it to the rim or dish it to the 2 or 3. If no one open and the lane blocked, the 1 then reserves with the ball and drives around the perimeter to the right wing. The 5 trails and sets a pick for the 1 to return to the center of the lane and rolls off to the right wing. It becomes a two person pick and roll on the right. This is highly effective against a man to man as the defense is overloaded on the left side, and if they aren't, then the 2 would have been open.

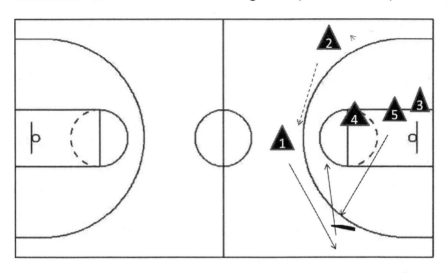

The Money Pick & Roll (1-4) is for the 4 to be ready to set another pick for the 1 after he or she comes off the 1-5 pick if the 1 is not able to get a free path to the basket or dish to another player.

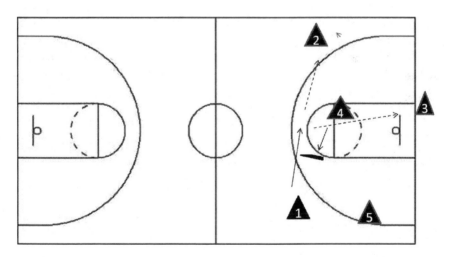

CHAPTER 14

---■---

Mongoose System – Secondary Break

The secondary break truly already began when no one was open on the initial rush up the court and the 1, in going through their progressions found neither the 3-2-5-4 players open and could not take it to the rim. However, when the 2 runs around, and if the player gets the ball, the first option for the 2 is to, of course, shoot, and if overplayed, cross step and drive. However, if these cannot be executed upon, then the 2 looks just as they did on the right wing, first to the 3 down low and next to the 4 at the left elbow. If those aren't there, then back to the 1.

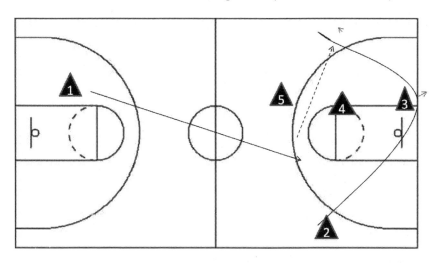

The 1 then takes the ball and creates space after the pick from the 5 on top and moves again to deep in the backcourt and the 2 and 3 then "wheel" as in the **Grinnell System** towards the ball and use picks from the 5 and 4 and the 1 looks hard as they rotate around the far side.

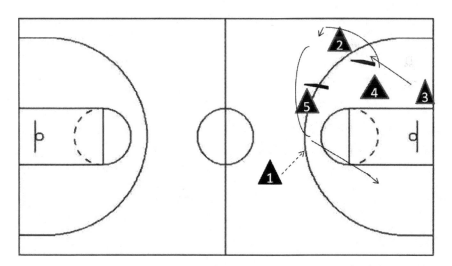

The other option to present to your opponents is our simplified Olivet. For details on all the options presented by the Mount Olivet Nazarene offense, go to the Bible on the **System**, **The Complete Guide to Coaching the System**. At this level, we believe simple is the only way to go in executing your team's offense in the **Mongoose System**. What we suggest to you is if and when your opponents are able to frustrate your attack and are able to anticipate your moves you can use this alternate progression, we, as an homage, call it Olivet. In this alignment, the 3 sets up at the left wing, the 5 runs the length of the court to where the 3 had set up, the 4 lines up at the right elbow instead of the left elbow, and the 1 takes the ball directly down the center of the court. Again, the 1 is looking 3-2-5-4 to deliver the ball. If the 2 is not open, he or she is to immediately go around the court to the left corner using a pick from the 5. The 1 is to look and deliver the ball quickly, again to whomever is open and use the correct progressions.

If no one is open the 4 is to move to the left elbow and set picks on top of the perimeter for the 1 as he or she drives towards the basket looking for a shot or a dish.

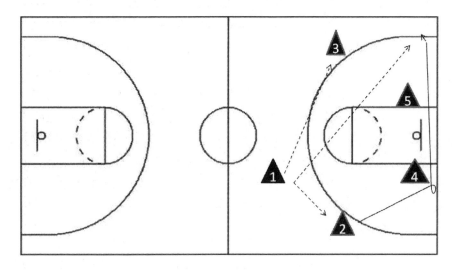

CHAPTER 15

■

Delay Game

You can't really slow down the **Mongoose System** once you have unleashed it and you will have indoctrinated your team to sprint all the time and when you try and shift into a "walk it up" tempo, we have found the energy just drains out of their bodies and creates confusion in their minds. Believe me, we have tried! However, at this age and development, specifically with the limited practice times you will be burdened with, we highly recommend you adopt a full "4 Corners" delay if you want to protect a lead towards the end of the game.

Our version of the 4 Corners is as follows. We suggest you, as always, get the ball to your 1. The 1 takes it down the dead middle of the court with your 2 and 3 set up in your opponents' end at the mid-court line and your 4 and 5 set up in the corners by the base line. Then, the 1 comes down and passes it to one of the players in the corner when they get approached by your opponent. The person receiving the pass moves with the ball towards the middle of the court looking to avoid your opponents. The person who passed the ball then moves behind the person they threw the ball to, ready to receive a pass. Rinse, and repeat...

No one is looking for a shot. It is keep-away and constant moving so your players maintain the same energy level of movement they had in the **Mongoose System.**

Your opponents will be thoroughly confused when you break into the 4 Corners as they have themselves been conditioned through the game that you will be looking basket, from anywhere (in their eyes), within 12 seconds of getting the ball. Many times, we have seen 30 to 45 seconds melt off the clock before our opponents have mentally recovered from this tactic and scream at the their players to foul and then call a time out and switch to a hard pressing half court or man defense, but then it's too late for them. In some cases, the other team has been so fatigued by the pace of the game that they are physically incapable of setting up a trap and their players (and sometimes coaches) are noticeably broken. And if our opponents shift into a man, we have given the green light for layups, ONLY, to our players if they have the opening.

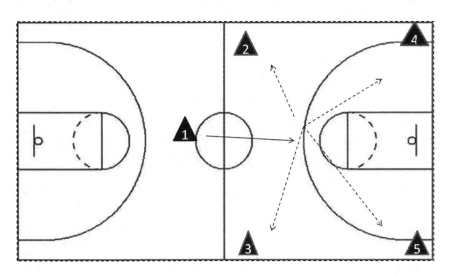

Now, I'll be frank. This tactic is <u>not</u> Coach Karen's favorite! It is <u>not</u> some of our parents when we go into it when we are only up 5 or 6 points with a minute to go. For them, it's nail biting time! We only have gotten into it within the last two minutes of games when we were up several points, or when up with only seconds to go.

However, if you have your finishing 5 on the floor and they have practiced this repetitively during practice, it will be a successful closer for you if you choose to use it. You will know if your team can do this and whether it should be implemented by watching how they do in practice. This is not for a Mercury program to try, but necessary for more experienced programs to have in their bag. Practice of it begins with 5 on 3 defenders and then adding one and then another until you actually practice it against six opponents.

CHAPTER 16

■

Out of bounds plays

Is there an original out of bounds play? I mean a play **no one** has ever come up with already? I guess it's possible. I don't know the origins of ours at this point; I just know these are plays that work. And what I mean by that is that we are consistently able to (1) in-bound the ball; and (2) get either a shot from the block or an open 3 point shot. We are attacking in our out of bounds plays, all the time.

We have found the key to their effectiveness is the repetition of them in practice and our 1 knowing and executing the proper pass & fake pass progressions, every time. In the Toy Soldier, our players line up in a stack in front of the ball. The 2 breaks away from the basket, the 5 breaks to the opposite block, the 3 breaks straight towards the ball and the 4 retreats behind the 3 point line as a safety valve option. The key is the 1 faking hard to the 2, and moving the defender in front of him or her away from the basket. If the defender takes the fake, the 3 will be open. If the 3 is not open, the 1 is to look to the 5 and then back to the 2. If no one is open, the 3 is to shield the defender to the inside and take a pass from the 1 and the 1 then steps onto the court and uses the shield for a midrange jumper.

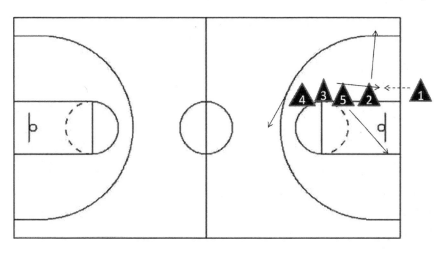

Our Picket Fence play is lined up as seen below. The play begins with the 2 running around the fence calling for the ball. The 1 fakes the pass to the 2, and then looks for the 3 cutting towards the ball again. The key if for the 3 to wait until the 2 has passed the fence before moving. The 5, again, cuts to the opposite block, and the 4 then retreats to the safety value spot again.

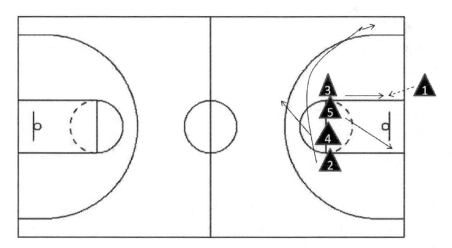

Our St. Peter play is designed to be run after running the first two above plays which have our opponents looking for us to attack the near block. All the players line up in a stack away from the ball. The 5 cuts to the near block and attempts to wedge a position in front of the defender, and if successful, the 5 should get the ball. If not, the 1 fakes and then fakes to the 2 who has cut all the way to the corner, ball side. The key to this play is the 1's ability to sell the play to the 5 and 2. This is because the 3 who began running with the 2 and 5, makes a sharp cut at the elbow and sprints back to the far block. Many times, at the middle school and youth levels, you can tell if this will be successful even before it starts because your opponents will not man the far block. This failure will be your manna, as they will not react in time to this misdirection. The 4 again retreats as a safety valve receiver.

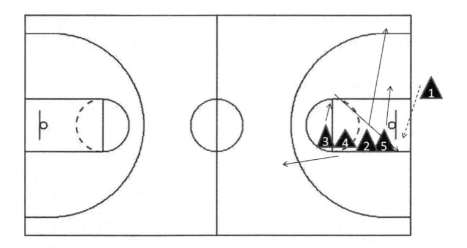

In Mercy, we line up four across. The 2 and 5 are always ball side. The 1, as quarterback, calls stay or go. On stay, the 1 throws a quick pass to the 2 or 3 as the 1 has seen them immediately open for a quick 3 pointer. On go, the 5 and 4 call repeatedly for the ball as they retreat to the elbows. The key is the 1 selling that he or she will try and throw the ball to them over a defender's head that was stationed on the blocks. The idea is to encourage them to take a step or two back. When the 4 and 5 retreat, the 2 and 3 race straight into the blocks and if they get between the defender and the basket, they receive the pass and shoot. The 5 and 4 circle back to where the 2 and 3 were if no one was open to get the ball into play.

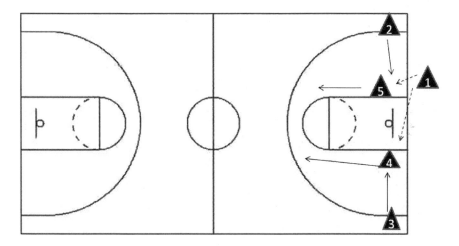

In Hickory, the 2 and 3 line up ball side and 4 and 5 on the far block and elbow. The 3 cuts across the lane and the 3, 4 and 5 set up a fence which the 2 races around and 1 then lobs the ball to the open area on top of the key that the 2 has raced to reach. The 2 guns a 3 pointer. The play is designed to be used in critical points in the game after we have set up our opponents in the above plays to look for us to be running a play that attacks the blocks and so the top of the key will be vulnerable and we want our best 3 point shooter to be in the launch position.

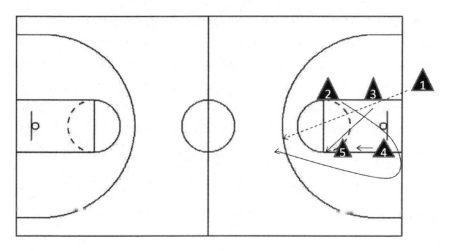

In Lion King, again the 2 and 3 are ball side. The idea is the person who sets a pick will not be considered a target by the defense. It starts with the 4 picking for the 5 who slides to the far block. In the meantime, the 3 has cut across the lane and positions him or her to pick for the 4. The 4 then cuts back off this pick towards the near block. The 1 has looked to the 5 and then the 4 at the blocks and if not there, the 2 makes a nice safety valve option outside the 3 point line.

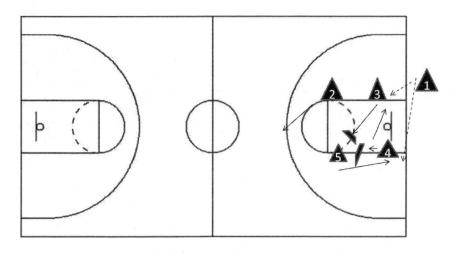

When we get the ball on the sideline, we almost always set up in our Picket Fence on the side. The 2 is always farthest from the basket and the 3 is closest. Next to the 3 is the 5 and then the 4. It is the same movement as under the basket except we are looking first for the 2, and if open getting the ball to him or her for a shot. If not, the 1 is to get the ball to the 3 or 5 and then receive the ball in return and attack the basket with the 2.

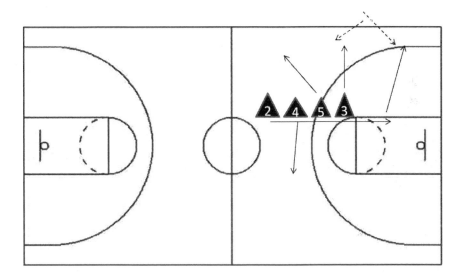

Our second sideline play is Yellow Submarine. This is the only play that our 5 throws the ball in from either the sideline or baseline. The 5 first looks to the 2 breaking towards the near wing. If open, we take a quick hitter 3 pointer. If not, the second option is to hit the 1 who broke off a pick set by the 4. Once the 1 gets it, he or she looks right back to the 2 if open. If not, the 5 has used a pick from the 3 and races to the far elbow. 1 then passes to the 5 quickly. If not open, either, then the 1 "runs to daylight," on either side of the 4. This play works well when there is ten seconds left. It can be run with five seconds as well but the 1 must move without hesitation.

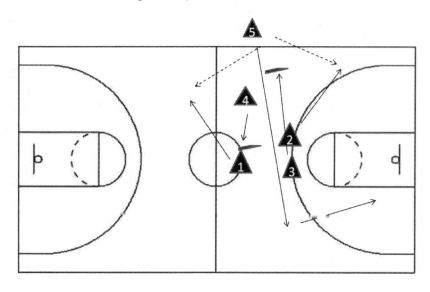

In Gideon, the players line up similarly to Picket Fence, but slightly different, and this difference is imperceptible to you opponents. The key is the rotation off the fence. Instead of running towards the basket, the 3 and then after a second the 2 following, race around the fence away from the basket using the 5 as a pick. The 1 looks to hit the first one open for a 3 pointer. A play to be used with less than five seconds left is Gideon.

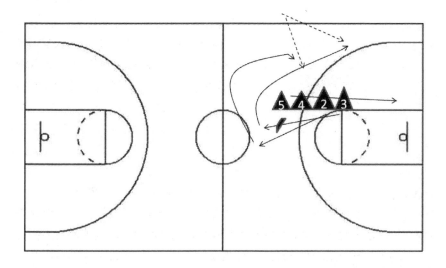

CHAPTER 17

■

Pressure defense

If you are going to commit to playing the **Mongoose System,** you <u>must</u> press. You <u>must</u> press the entire game. It is not an option if you are going to utilize your players' potential to their capacity. If your local rules do not permit pressing or only limited pressing, you still can exercise a pressure defensive scheme at half court. However, whenever possible, you will need to use the whole court to apply incessant pressure.

This will maximize your players ability to disrupt your opponents attack and by doing so, add to their physical state of fatigue while breaking them mentally. Your rotation becomes central to the success of this scheme and the longer the game runs, the better your pressure will become as your opponents will use the same couple of ball handlers to bring the rock down the court and you will be placing fresher trappers in their face.

In the beginning of the game, your opponents may break your press more often and this is not the time to panic or change strategies, because they will break down. And, when your opponents have that moment of crisis, you will have an opportunity for three to four baskets during it.

This is more so at the middle school and youth levels than the higher levels because players at this level do not have depth of mental toughness to withstand a steal or turnover and then immediately shake it off.

In full court, we use a 2-2-1 press, which we call UCLA – after the Wooden 2-2-1 press. However, different than their application, we put our 3 and 4 down as our trappers. They are to allow the ball to be thrown into play in front of them and then trap the ball. The 1 and 2 get into the passing lanes of the two players nearest to the ball anticipating as interceptors. Their objective is to get a steal or force our opponents to turn the ball over due to the pressure. Our 5 is the safety, but we want our 5 to not be passive and attempt to quickly seek to close on long passes and intercept them or at a minimum, disrupt them.

Our 4 is usually our slowest reacting player on defense and plays on the weak hand side of our opponents point guard. Generally, as their point is right-handed, our 4 plays on our right in the trap, as our 3 is less susceptible to the speed dribble when they try to break the press. We almost universally use this press as our initial press and when we have a twelve person squad or more, rotate three sets of 3 and 4 pairs. When they are fresher, and force our opponents to truly work the ball up the court, our opponents will break.

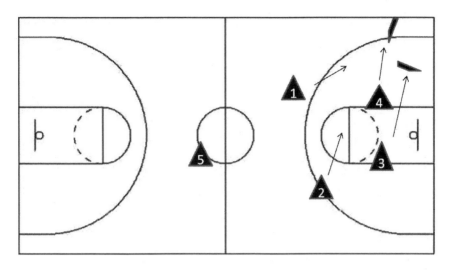

Our second main press is our 1-2-1-1 full court press. We call it Tech. We play it according to Hoyle. The 4 refuses an in-bounds pass to the center of the court, and does not cover the initial throw-in. This is a Coach Arseneault heresy as his teachings encourage pressure on the thrower. However, our goal is to trap the ball in one of the corners and we have found we need our 4 to be back further in order to effectively close the trap begun by our 1 or 3. When our 4, at this skill level, and with possible speed limitations, is all the way on the ball, it becomes too much distance to cover in order to effectively close the trap. Our 2 is to be our interceptor on any pass up the line and the far defender (either 1 or 3), move to be the interceptor in the middle of the court. It is imperative for you to teach your players to not cover "air" and be hungry to get and control the passing lanes. Our 1 lines up on our opponent's point guard's strong side, which again, at this level, most ball handlers have a definite strong and weak side and their speed up the court with their weak hand is remarkably compromised and so it's best to have your most agile trapper on the strong side.

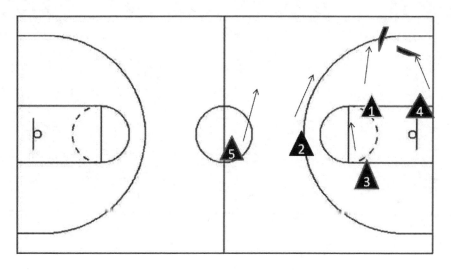

We use a Blitz press, a simple form of it fashioned after Coach Morgan Wooten's. We add this press after the Mercury program. It is a weapon we rarely begin a game with and instead wait until halftime to switch into it so as to not allow our opponents to react at the long break and force them to use a timeout attempt to address it in that short span.

In the Blitz, our 3 and 4 cover and aggressively deny the in-bounds throw to our opponent's two best ball handlers. If they have trouble, and our opponents have one superstar, we will double that star with our 1 and 3 and then once the ball goes to our opponent's second option, our 1 then races over to trap with the 4. Our 3 stays in man coverage versus the star and aggressively denies the ball. Our 2 shifts to cover the "near man" to the ball after initially setting up as denying his or her mark the initial pass. The 2 has to hustle and get in that next passing lane. In any case, the 1 jumps into a trap against whomever gets the ball thrown to them. The 5 gets ultra-aggressive looking for passing lanes and sometimes leaves the safety position if an opportunity to finish the play for a turnover occurs.

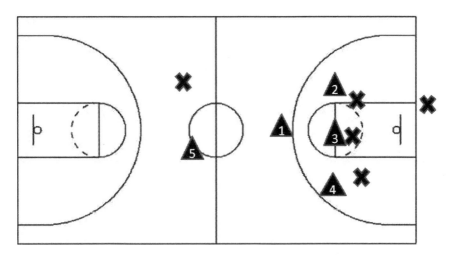

We also can get into a ¾ press we call City, when after a made basket. The goal is for our 4 to slide the ball into the trapping sides of the court. Our 1 slides to deny a pass from the corner to the wing and the far side defender slides to the center of the court. The 5 is the safety. If you are playing a team that consistently has the same depth and speed as you do, you may find this as a valuable pressure tool. Your 4 is to apply enough pressure after the throw-in to not allow the ball handler to get a complete look at the court and your opponents to fill the holes of your zone without challenge. Again, your players cannot cover air and must quickly shift into the passing lanes.

On a missed basket, we have our players run to these same pre-assigned positions and we call this our Zulu press. Many opponents will believe we are getting back and try and use this as an opportunity to try and slow the game down or catch a breath. However, in actuality, they are only giving us the needed time to set up this ¾ trap.

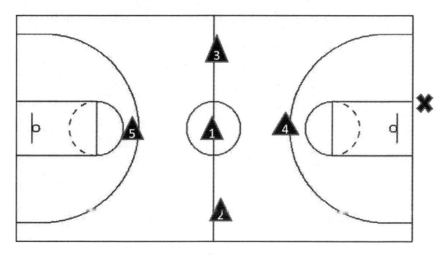

If using the City or Zulu, you can easily withdraw, in an orderly fashion into a 1-3-1 half court defense. We call ours Maltese Cross. It is to promote half court trapping wherever we can. The 1 becomes the chief interceptor and is encouraged to take chances in the passing lanes.

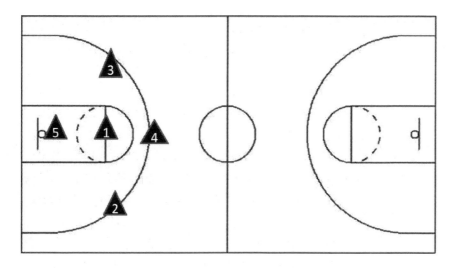

We teach our players to also run a 1-2-2 half court defense. Our 4 is the "Mongoose" and the 4 follows the ball all around the perimeter. The 1 and 3 are to cover the ball wherever it goes on their side of the court and the 2 and 5 stay on their blocks and do <u>not</u> wander out towards the corner and oppose a shot from there. It requires a lot of running by the 1, 2 and 3 and again your rotation must account for this if you choose this in half court.

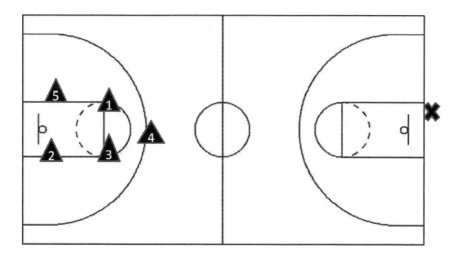

The Mongoose gives you one more immediate rebounder around the rim if you are having trouble with the Maltese Cross. The next step we have taken is the Box and 1, or Freak. This defense maintains a man to man on their "superstar" and can be matched up by our 3 or 2 (or even 1), depending on the shift. The key is the "freak" player. In the diagram below, the freak is the 3, and their job is to run to the side of the ball. The 3 cannot overrun the play and is giving up the quick swing around the perimeter 3 pointer. Whomever is covering the star, must deny the ball at all times and if you began in a Blitz full court press, this may be an option for you to retreat into because you are telling your team, and your opponents, the other four players are going to have to beat you. The other three players form a triangle and rotate to the side of the ball, but stay "paint heavy" in order to try and clean every rebound from the boards.

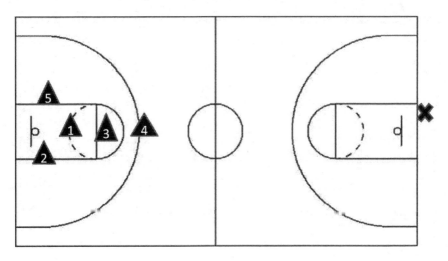

Whenever our opponent has a dead ball under our basket, we set up in a modified 2-3 defense. We have our 4 set up out wide to deny a quick hitter 3 pointer. Our 5 is on the ball side block and stays at home, denying a shot from there. Our 1 is in the middle of the two blocks in the paint. Our 2 sets up on the far side block and denies any shot from this spot. Our 3 roams in the paint, and first denies any pass to the ball side elbow and center of the paint. We are forcing our opponent to work the ball from the back court or take a long shot, but refusing all high percentage shooting locations, period.

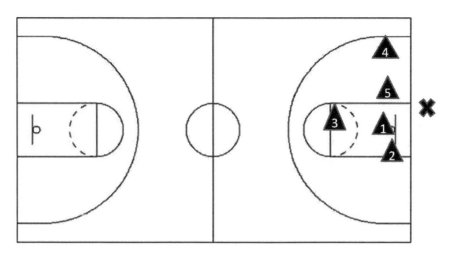

The final word is that in the **Mongoose System**, we don't run a full man defense, and choose to switch and trap the length of the court. Don't ask the impossible of your players on defense and be sure to adjust into whichever one suits your personnel best. You don't need Jason and the Argonauts or Amazons to run this defense, you just need to practice the fundamentals, over and over again and then rotate your players generously. Patience is the ingredient you must never leave home without as your opponents will break your press, and sometimes, frequently. Discuss during the game, with your players, not "at" them, the fundamentals they must focus on to begin to break your opponents.

CHAPTER 18

■

Press Breaks

Let's start with this. You WANT them to press YOU, too! You want their team to never rest. Although the stakes get higher and your chances for making your own turnovers go up when your opponent presses, if you prepare well and practice thoroughly your own press breaks, they will be hoisted on their own petard by pressing you!

Our number one press break we call LMU, an homage to Coach Westhead and his historic team there. We line up all our players on the foul line in front of the throw-in. The 1 cuts diagonally towards the ball, not waiting for any of our other players to even line up, and gets the ball as soon as possible. The 2 lines up in his or her lane on the right side of the court and the 3 lines up on the left side. The 4 lines up on the elbow in front of the ball and sets pick for the 1 after the 1 receives the ball. The second option for the 5, who _always_ throws it in, is to hit the 2 who has done a break towards midcourt and then a sharp cut back to the center of the lane. If the 2 gets it, they are to pivot and look for the 1 streaking past. If those options are not there, the 5 is to look for the 3. The 3 has broke to midcourt and then reversed and headed straight back in a line towards our baseline. If the 3 gets the ball, they also look to the 1 who has, by now slanted across the court and will be in position up court before the 3.

The keys to this break are the 1 constantly looking to the ball, whoever hands it is in, and going north and south with the ball once in his or her possession. The 5 being trained to run the line to be able to make the easiest inbounds pass, on a made basket, and not to be shackled in place. And three, the 1 quickly setting up and cutting, and others before opponents get organized into their press.

The 1 <u>must</u> be in motion when catching the ball in order to get inertia rolling to help avoid the quick trap, and be prepared to run opponents over who are caught "blocking" because they are without time to get set in defensive position. The LMU is *most* favored by us, because if our opponents want to cover tightly, they commit themselves to a full court running game in order to even attempt to prevent us from getting the in play. Not *mate*, but certainly, "*check!*"

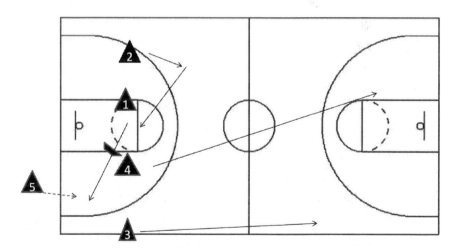

The Puff is our second press break. It is one we employ against a 1-2-1-1 when we are having difficulty in our LMU.

It is designed to quickly pass the ball to the 1 up the court after a throw-in to the 2, 3, or 4. The 1 races to the side of the court that the 5 throws the ball to, in a slight slant, towards the initial receiver whose job it is to pivot quickly and look to the 1.

If the 1 is not open, the initial receiver may turn and dribble up the court, if not double teamed. If in trouble, the receiver is to look back to the 5 who then reverses the court with a quick pass. This reversal receiver can hen dribble up the court taking advantage of the delay in the press to adjust and rotate, or pass ahead to the 1.

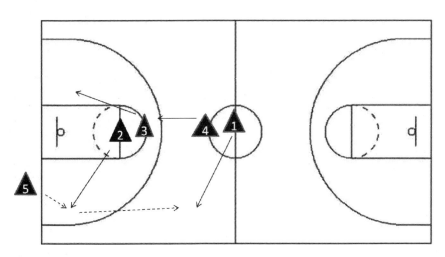

Our third break, which we only teach after using the LMU and Puff is Jailbreak. The reason we do this third is because the first two force our opponents to immediately commit all the way on our end of the court to apply pressure, and Jailbreak does allow them to start back at midcourt. Also, it takes the ball out of our 1's hands almost immediately and in **Mercury** and **Gemini**, we may not have enough effective ball handlers to run this effectively.

It begins with the 1 doing the same cut as in LMU, and then making a quick pass to the 3 who cuts back towards the top of the key. Once received, the 3 then dribbles the ball down the court in an attempt to force a 3 on 2 fast break. If the 3 is not open, the 1 looks quickly to the 2 or tries to shorten the distance to the 4 who is posted on the opposite side of the court. If either player receives the ball, their job is to go with the ball in their lane forcing the play upon the opposition each running to their **Mongoose System** shooting spots.

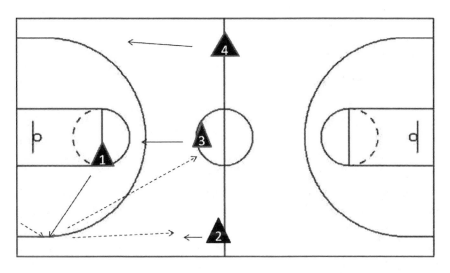

Finally, the OOCLA break can be used at the lowest level of organization and we have used it when working with very young youth level teams, and we teach it in order to prepare our players to defend against it as many teams use a break that incorporates a "pass back" to their 1. OOCLA is our only break that has our 1 throw the ball in. The 2 and 3 cut towards the ball just as in Puff, and the 5 breaks back to the foul line looking for the ball. The 4 is a decoy and runs down the court.

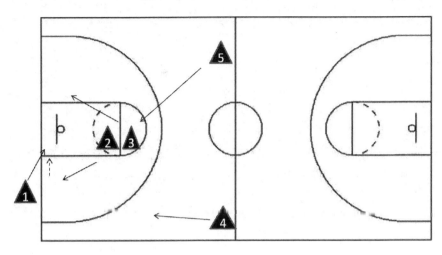

You must teach your players to love being pressed. It will change their whole dynamic about the pressure other teams are attempting to apply. It's more than them "embracing the horror" of rabid dogs nipping at their heels. It's getting your players to buy into the idea that they aren't being trapped in the back court, **<u>your opponents are!</u>** They will be foolishly chasing your players and have to foul you to even slow you down. Convince them of the truth, that most teams do <u>not</u> press the entire game and are not physically fit enough to do it. Nor are your opponents capable due to their lack of confidence in their full team's capability. On T.V., they'd call it the bench, and the coach doesn't have confidence in his or her bench players. However, with the **Mongoose System**, there …is…no…bench.

CHAPTER 19

■

Game Time Strategy & Adjustments

How to start the game is not anything like how you will need to finish the game. We <u>don't</u> have "starters." We have our first shift that takes the court and then rotate as quickly as the rules allow. Our druthers are to rotate each minute. So at the 45 second mark of each minute, our subs go the scorer's table ready to go into the game. Sometimes they go in early and other times they aren't able to enter until the shift on the court plays for 1:15.

The patience to wait on adjustments on defense is critical to success during the game. As stated above, your team may not look effective early in the press, but your players will wear your opponents down throughout the game causing turnovers.

To be, or not to be, that is the question? Or in this context, to call time out or not – that IS the question? Whenever you call time out early, you give your opponents time to rest. Please avoid calling timeouts even when there is a small run against your team. I know that sounds heretical, but you can effectively save your timeouts for critically important strategic situations and for saving the ball when a player is in trouble and thus avoid losing a possession.

Does anyone miss a rotation? Yes, if you say so. If you need to sit a player due to discipline, fatigue, or they simply have been broken for whatever reason during the game, you have the authority to do so. We have done this for all these reasons and your coaching staff must closely watch your players before the game and during it to assess whether players need to sit out a shift or not. Players may not always honestly tell you how they are doing and want to stay in the even when they are spent.

CHAPTER 20

Offensive Set Plays
in your Pocket

Picking a couple simple set plays for your team to use gives you the flexibility to pull them out of your pocket in a critical moment in the game. It also will give your offense a new look that your opponents won't anticipate. We don't recommend spending too much time having your players memorize numerous set plays at this level, but a couple are a healthy medicine. These may be needed when you have dead ball situations late in the game and your opponents have had the chance to completely set up their defense. Again, you don't need any set plays for the **Mongoose System** to be effective, <u>**at all!**</u> Here, below are some options we suggest to you with our own play names:

Travis   vs. 1-3-1 or 1-2-2

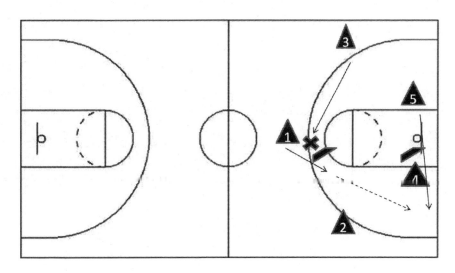

Alcindor   vs. half court trap 1-2-2

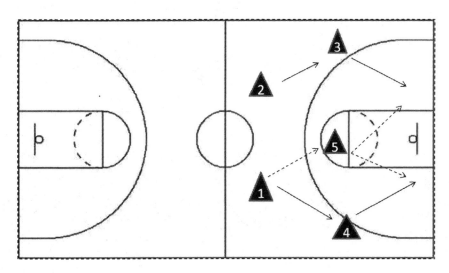

Eagle   vs. 1-2-2 or man

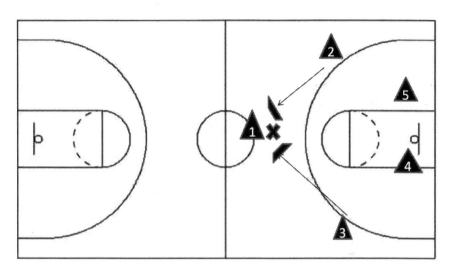

Shaq   vs. 1-2-2 or man or 1-3-1

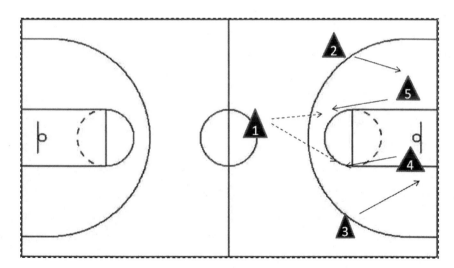

Boudreau   vs. 1-2-2 or man or 1-3-1

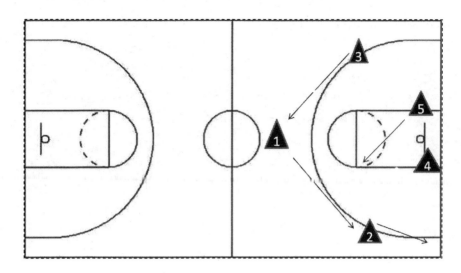

Jimmer   vs. 1-2-2 or man

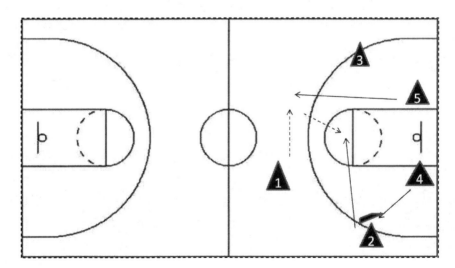

Kentucky   vs. 1-2-2 or man or 1-3-1

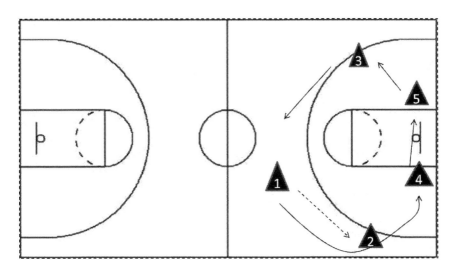

CHAPTER 21

◼

The Bigger the court...
the bigger the opportunity

The **Mongoose System** is made for the biggest courts and showcases at the middle school and youth tournaments. This is because when your team is built to run, and your opponent is not, you have an advantage. Even when they are used to running, their best ball handlers will not be used to pressure all the time. Also, even if they are used to running and pressure, your opponents will be worn down by your rotation throughout the game. This philosophy is magnified on bigger courts and stages when you unleash your team's natural youthful exuberance and run the anxiety of the moment out of them.

"Fatigue makes cowards of us all." Coach Lombardi used to tell his players that and we tell our players the same thing. When our opponents get tired they hesitate, make errors and eventually break. We run hard every practice, and in teaching the whole, we attempt to place our players in game simulations even in drills whenever possible. The more they feel it by using music, game noise, a game clock and even our own small scoreboard prepares them for the big show. You can now get a decent scoreboard with a place to hook you iPod or phone into for under $200.

Practice in preparation of big courts if you only have access to a small gym or sometimes a half court at your disposal. You must have your players execute passes and runs from as far distant as possible to enable success in the **Mongoose System**. This can be logistically difficult based on your resources at your school or league. Most youth leagues limit practice times and space. You can do this with limited space, but you must be cognizant of how large the courts you play on will be and run your practices accordingly.

There will always be detractors of the **System**, and especially the **Mongoose System**. They will come out of the stands and may even be your own AD until they buy into it. Sometimes they never will, but you have an obligation as their coach to teach each player not only how to play, but how they can love the game through this approach. When your players love the game, they will practice more, practice on their own, and do all the things they will need to do to be the best they can be. Finally, your time with your players is fleeting, and you must do the most you can for them as their coach, and the **Mongoose System** gives them the best chance to improve, individually and as a team. The greatest gift you can receive, as a coach at this level, is in knowing you have taught life lessons to kids and take pride when they love the game and continue to play, maybe even at the next level!

The top of the Wooden Pyramid is "Competitive Greatness." Playing your best when your best is needed how Coach Wooden describes it. The **Mongoose System** doesn't just allow players to play their best, it frees them to go beyond what even they though could be their best. It is a championship vehicle for your team and your middle school's program if you can teach it to them. The more years your players participate in it, the more they can work on it and the fundamentals that are imperative to its success. These same principles will give your players a leg up on playing at the next level in high school.

Your team can achieve championships in tournaments and leagues by using the **Mongoose System** & playing everyone on the team. There is no greater feeling in sports when all members on the squad contribute with their gifts to achieve a title. Coach Lombardi said, "the measure of a person is what he or she does with the gifts and talents they have." We are giving each player on your team the chance to maximize the gifts they bring to your team's spirit and promise when you choose to employ the **Mongoose System.** Are you ready to win your next championship? We think you are!

APPENDIX 1

Rotations

1st Quarter

6:00	5:00	4:00	3:00	2:00	1:00
1 Snoopy	Downtown Casey	Snoopy	Downtown Casey	Snoopy	Downtown Casey
2 Princess	Bear	Princess Sarah	Bear	Princess	Bear
3 Rudy	Tigger	Bear	Rudy	Tigger	Sarah Bear
4 Mushu	Smurfette	Tiger Lilly	Mushu	Smurfette	Tiger Lilly
5 Ethyl	Maddie	Ethyl	Maddie	Ethyl	Maddie

2nd Quarter

6:00	5:00	4:00	3:00	**2:00**	**1:00**
1 Snoopy	Downtown Casey	Snoopy	Downtown Casey	**Snoopy**	**Downtown**
2 Princess	Bear	Princess Sarah	Bear	**Princess**	**Tigger**
3 Rudy	Tigger	Bear	Rudy	**Sarah Bear**	**Rudy**
4 Mushu	Smurfette	Tiger Lilly	Mushu	**Tiger Lilly**	**Mushu**
5 Ethyl	Maddie	Ethyl	Maddie	**Ethyl**	**Maddie**

3rd Quarter

6:00	5:00	4:00	3:00	2:00	1:00
1 Snoopy	Downtown Casey	Snoopy	Downtown Casey	Snoopy	Downtown Casey
2 Princess	Bear	Princess	Bear	Princess	Bear

	Sarah			Sarah		
3	Bear	Rudy	Tigger	Bear	Rudy	Tigger
	Tiger			Tiger Lilly		
4	Lilly	Mushu	Smurfette		Mushu	Smurfette
5	Ethyl	Maddie	Ethyl	Maddie	Ethyl	Maddie

4th Quarter

	6:00	5:00	4:00	3:00	2:00	1:00
1	Snoopy	Downtown Casey	Snoopy	Downtown	Snoopy	Snoopy
2	Princess	Bear	Princess Sarah	Tigger	Downtown	Princess
3	Rudy	Tigger	Bear	Rudy	Rudy Casey	Downtown
4	Mushu	Smurfette	Tiger Lilly	Mushu	Bear	Rudy
5	Maddie	Ethyl	Maddie	Ethyl	Maddie	Maddie

APPENDIX 2

—■—

Seasonal Stats

2012-13 STM CSAL Boys Basketball Record: 19-12

(FINAL Statistics through season)

Player	Points	Shots	Made FG	FG %	Rebounds	Steals	Point Leader
Brandon	178	225	77	34%	50	95	13
Clayton	150	199	51	26%	40	41	5
Jacob	79	126	33	26%	64	35	1
Murphy	34	69	13	19%	113	23	0
Grant	58	105	25	24%	112	31	1
SUBTOTAL	496	727	199	27%	379	225	20
Landon	140	209	52	25%	165	63	5
Brock	185	296	68	23%	67	44	9
Joseph	60	104	24	23%	42	22	0
Stephen	39	62	17	27%	93	24	0
Greg	44	47	15	32%	64	17	1
SUBTOTAL	470	718	178	25%	431	170	15
TOTALS	966	1445	377	26%	810	395	n/a
Average per game	31	47	12	26%	26	13	n/a

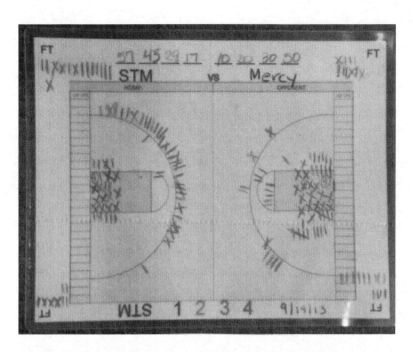

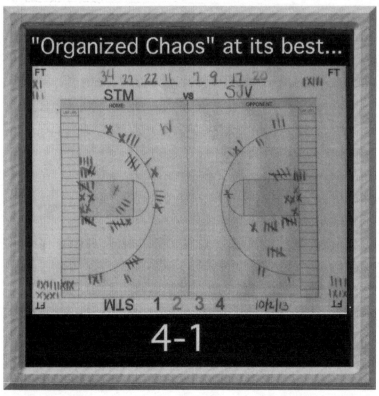

"Organized Chaos" at its best...

4-1

CSAL

21 GAMES

Record 10-11

Player	Points	Att. FG	Made FG	FG %	3 pt Shot Att.	3 pt Shot Made	3 pt Shot %	Point Leader # games
Casey	56	96	16	17%	64	5	8%	4
Maddie	55	53	14	26%	4	4	100%	6
Elise	47	91	10	11%	25	7	28%	4
Jansen	40	28	3	11%	74	11	15%	4
Ashley	37	65	18	28%	14	1	7%	3
Emma	27	64	5	8%	47	4	9%	2
Emily	15	68	7	10%	1	0	0%	1
Kandace	14	31	6	19%	4	0	0%	0
Vivian	14	17	6	35%	1	0	0%	0
Sarah	4	18	2	11%	0	0	---	0
Emme	4	22	1	5%	0	0	---	0
Lillie	1	10	0	0%	0	0	---	0
TOTALS	314	563	88	16%	234	32	14%	------
Average per game	15	27	4	16%	11	2	14%	------

YMCA

8 GAMES

Record 6-2

Player	Points	Att. FG	Made FG	FG %	3 pt Shot Att.	3 pt Shot Made	3 pt Shot %	Point Leader # games
Casey	35	18	4	22%	40	7	18%	1
Maddie	26	19	4	21%	42	5	12%	3
Elise	29	32	12	38%	13	1	8%	2
Jansen	----	----	----	----	----	----	----	----
Ashley	39	18	2	11%	42	11	26%	4
Emma	----	----	----	----	----	----	----	----
Emily	20	32	10	31%	1	0	0%	0
Kandace	10	20	4	20%	4	0	0%	0
Vivian	13	12	5	42%	2	1	50%	0
Sarah	16	18	8	44%	0	0	---	1
Emme	13	21	6	29%	1	0	0%	0
Lillie	2	7	1	14%	0	0	---	0
TOTALS	205	176	56	32%	145	25	17%	------
Average per game	26	22	7	32% WOW	18	3	17%	------

Total   15 Wins - 5 Losses

	2PT		3PT		FT		Pts	OR	TO	SD	2PT	3PT	FT	FG %
	M	A	M	A	M	A					%	%	%	%
Ashley	14 of 68		22 of 138		14 of 46		108	15	48		21%	16%	30%	17%
Casey	8 of 61		29 of 137		22 of 48		107	15	52		13%	17%	46%	16%
Elise	24 of 94		6 of 64		17 of 56		83	23	63		26%	9%	30%	19%
Emily	25 of 73		0 of 0		6 of 15		56	35	25		34%	0%	40%	34%
Emma	12 of 72		1 of 7		10 of 43		37	37	28		17%	14%	23%	16%
Emme	4 of 17		0 of 2		0 of 2		8	11	10		24%	0%	0%	21%
Jansen	0 of 12		29 of 146		4 of 12		91	4	17		0%	20%	33%	18%
Kandace	5 of 32		1 of 9		5 of 10		18	25	15		16%	11%	50%	15%
Lillie	1 of 16		0 of 0		1 of 5		3	6	17		6%	0%	20%	6%
Maddie	24 of 110		9 of 43		12 of 31		87	68	33		22%	21%	39%	22%
Sarah	7 of 26		0 of 1		1 of 2		15	24	15		27%	0%	50%	26%
Vivian	8 of 49		0 of 5		7 of 24		23	56	29		16%	0%	29%	15%
TOTAL	132 of 630		91 of 552		99 of 294		636	339	352	287				

| % | 21% | | 16% | | 34% | | | | | | | | | |
| Shooting | | | 19% | | | | | | | | | | | |

Matrix   45 5 + 22 3's + 33% OR + 12 SD + 16 TO's = W

1182 552   35%   14   18

APPENDIX 3

Forms

Tryout Questionnaire   Y/N/NA?#

1. Did you play school basketball ball last year? _____

2. Did you play off-season basketball once? _____

3. Did you play off-season basketball more than once? _____

4. Did you ever play school basketball in 6th or 7th grade? _____

5. Do you play a regular position, and what number? _____

6. Do you know what the "System" offense is? _____

7. Do you know what a full court press defense is? _____

8. Is this your only out of school commitment this fall? _____

9. Do you know you are guaranteed to play zero minutes? _____

10. Are you familiar with our basketball playbook? _____

Tryouts Skills Ratings (1-5 with 5 being the best)

1. Dribbling _____
2. Shooting (short range) _____
3. Free Throws _____
4. Lay ups _____
5. Defensive Stance & foot work _____
6. Passing & Receiving a pass _____
7. Rebounding _____
0. 3 Point Shooting _____
9. Hustle _____
10. Speed _____

TOTAL (OUT OF 50 POSSIBLE) _____

2013 SCHOOL Girls' BASKETBALL

Player Information Form and Questionnaire

1. **PLAYER'S NAME**_____

2. Parent's Names_____

3. Parent's cell _____

   _____

4. Favorite subject in school_____

5. When I grow up I want to be..._____

6. I would like to try and play this position(s)
   (number please)_____

7. I am prepared to do the following this summer to make myself a better player in the fall for our team (please circle all you are willing to do):

   Swimming team

   Jog

   Ride my bike

   Jump rope every week (at least once a week -- try and do this for 5 minutes and then build up to 15 minutes straight)

   Shoot 100 baskets a week (or more) from where you will be shooting on the court

Shoot 100 free throws a week

Dribble a basketball around the neighborhood once a week

Play catch with the basketball

Attend a basketball camp this summer

Read the Wooden book (first 90 pages) that Coach loaned you

8. Are you interested in possibly being a captain this fall?

   _____

9. What would you bring to the team as a leader if you were named captain?

   _____

   _____

   _____

10. What is your greatest strength you bring to the team?

    _____

11. What is your greatest weakness? What will you do this summer to overcome it?

    _____

    _____

12. Last fall we were a .500 ball club overall and won 10 games out of 21 and zero tournament trophies. How

many games do you expect us to win this fall? If more than ten wins, how do you think we can accomplish this, together?

_____

_____

_____

13. Do you think you have what it takes to play high school basketball, right now? If not, how could we help you improve this summer and fall, as a player, so you could play in high school?

_____

_____

SIGNATURE OF PLAYER_____

DATE:_____

_____

YEAR END PLAYER QUESTIONAIRE – BEFORE THE FINAL CHAMPIONSHIP WEEKEND

1. Why are you here?

2. What is your goal for this week?

3. What have been your favorite moments on this journey this past year?

4. What will you remember from this journey?

5. Have you learned anything from this journey? If so, what?

6. How does it feel to be a champion?

7. You are one of the 12...How have you mattered to our success?

APPENDIX 4

Coaching Templates

Mongoose System Basketball - Coaching Template

Primary Break

1 Drive
3 Long Pass
2 Three Pointer
2 Option
5 top of key
4 elbow

Secondary Break

2 runs around (2-3)
Iso Pick & Roll (1-5)
Money Pick & Roll (1-4)
Wheel

Out of Bounds

Toy Solider
Picket Fence

St. Peter
Mercy
Hickory
Gideon
Lion King
Yellow Submarine

Press Break

LMU
Puff
Jail Break

Press Defense

UCLA - 2-2-1
Tech - 1-2-1-1
Blitz
City
Pelican

Half Court Defense

Maltese Cross (1-3-1)
Mongoose (1-2-2)
Box & 1
Freak
2-3
Stand To (3-2)
Man to Man

Bench Coach Plus & Minus Chart - template

#	Player Name	Plus (+)	Minus (-)

OR =   Offensive rebound   A =   Assist

R =   Defensive rebound   (+) =   hustle play on offense or

S =   Steal   defense

TO =   Turnover   (-) =   failure to hustle on offense

2 =   made FG   or defense

3 =   made 3 point shot

Bibliography

Arseneault, David, *The Running Game*, Reedswain, Spring City, PA, 1997.

Arseneault, David, System Successes, Aresenault Productions, 2013.

Bergot, Erwan, *The Africa Korps*, Ballard, 1971, translated by Allan Wingate, New York, 1975.

Dale, Greg, Ph.D., Conant, Scott, M.A., *101 Teambuilding Activities: Ideas Every Coach Can Use to Enhance Teamwork, Communication and Trust,* Excellence in Performance, Durham, NC, 2004.

DeBerry, Fisher & Burrows, Mike, *The Power of Influence: Life-Changing Lessons from the Coach,* Fisher DeBerry Foundation, Colorado Springs, CO, 2009.

Gandolfi, Giorgio (editor), *NBA Coaches Playbook: Techniques, Tactics and Teaching Points*, Human Kinetics, Champaign, IL, 2009.

Gildea, William & Turan, Kenneth, *The Future is Now: George Allen, Pro Football's Most Controversial Coach,* Houghton Mifflin Co., 1972.

Greene, Robert, *The 33 Strategies of War*, Penguin, New York, 2006.

Kuchar, Bill, Kuchar, Mike, *Coaching High School Basketball: A Complete Guide to Building a Championship Team,* McGraw-Hill, New York, 2005.

May, Herbert G., Metzger, Bruce, M., (editors), *The New Oxford Annotated Bible with the Apocrypha, RSV,* Oxford University Press, New York, 1977.

Phillips, Donald T., *Run to Win: Vince Lombardi on Coaching and Leadership,* St. Martin's Press, New York, 2001.

Pierson, Carl J., *The Politics of Coaching: A Survival Guide to Keep Coaches from Getting Burned,* Double Nickel, 2011.

Ramsay, Jack, *Pressure Basketball,* Prentice-Hall, Englewood Cliffs, CA, 1965.

Sivils, Kevin, *Defending the Three-Point Shot,* Southern Family Publishing, Katy, TX, 2012.

Smith, Gary & Porter, Doug, *Coaching the System: A Complete Guide to Basketball's Most Explosive Style of Play,* RoundBall Productions, 2011.

Sorensen, Theodore C., *Let the Word Go Forth: The Speeches, Statements and Writings of John F. Kennedy, 1947-1963,* Delacorte, New York, 1988.

Ury, William, *The Power of a Positive No: How to Say No and Still Get to Yes,* Bantam Dell, New York, 2008.

Wooden, John, *Practical Modern Basketball (3d. Ed.),* Allyn & Bacon, Needham Heights, MA, 1999.

Wooden, John, Carty, Jay, *Coach Wooden's Pyramid of Success: Building Blocks for a Better Life,* Regal, Ventura, CA, 2005.

Wooden, John, Nater, Swen, *John Wooden's UCLA Offense,* Human Kinetics, Champaign, IL, 2006.

Wootten, Morgan, Gilbert, Dave, *Coaching Basketball Successfully (2d, Ed.),* Human Kinetics, Champaign, IL, 2003.

Videos

Basketball in the Fast Lane, Paul Westhead, Championship Productions (re-release 2010).

Coach Carter, (2005).

Grinnell Offense - Forcing Tempo, Dave Arseneault, Sysko's Sports Productions. (2008).

Grinnell Defense – Forcing Tempo, Dave Arseneault, Sysko's Sports Productions. (2008).

Guru of Go, Bill Couturie, Director, ESPN 30 for 30 Series, (2010).

The Heart of the Game, Ward Serrill, Director, Miramax Films, (2005).

Hoosiers, David Anspaugh, Director, Hemdale Film Corporation, (1986).

John Wooden's UCLA Offense, John Wooden, Swen Nater, Human Kinetics, (2006).

Lombardi, Ed Sabol, NFL Films Productions, (1968).

About the Authors

———————— ■ ————————

Beau James Brock

Beau was born in New Orleans, Louisiana and raised in Slidell, Louisiana, and Apple Valley, Minnesota. He is blessed to have five children Katherine 22, Lauren 20, Travis 15, James 13, and Tommy 10. He has coached boys and girls basketball, soccer and tennis, during different periods, over the last twenty years. He was active in high school sports as player at Apple Valley Senior High School as four year varsity letter winner in tennis and a two year letter winner in soccer also earning All-Conference and "Eagle" Award for leadership his senior year. He played high school basketball through his sophomore year, but focused on tennis and soccer his junior and senior years. He is a full-time practicing attorney and member of the Louisiana State Bar Association since 1991, a graduate of the Paul M. Hebert L.S.U. Law Center and L.S.U. for his undergraduate degree in history. He is currently in private practice and previously worked as an Assistant District Attorney, as an E.P.A. criminal attorney with federal agents to investigate environmental crimes, and at our state's environmental protection agency on its executive staff. He also has worked as a teacher and instructor for the past eighteen years for attorneys, law enforcement & paralegals. He was married for twenty-three years, but now is divorced.

L. Thomas Szekely

Thomas is currently employed as Vice President of a national relocation company. He has been a licensed CPA for the past fifteen years. His volunteer efforts have landed him roles as Junior Achievement instructor and currently a position on the Board of Directors for the YMCA. He is also a member of various professional organizations. He received his Bachelors of Science in Accounting from Louisiana State University and then furthered his education concentrating on Psychology and English Literature. He has participated in multiple sports throughout the years but today his main focus is on being an avid runner. His love for children and sports is what brought him to coaching. Over the past ten years, his attention has been on coaching girls' basketball, but recently has begun to coach boys as well. He was born in Baton Rouge, Louisiana and has resided in South Louisiana all of his life. He has two wonderful daughters Katelyn 17 and Madison 14.

Karen Recurt Kyler

Karen was born and raised in New Orleans, Louisiana. Straight from high school, she went to LSU School of Dentistry for the Dental Assisting Program and continued working there in the Oral & Maxillofacial Surgery Department for ten years and for an Endodontist (Root Canal Specialist) for an additional ten years. After marrying, she moved Baton Rouge in 1990, where she resides with her husband (an Orthodontist) and two daughters, Katelyn (19) and Kandace (14). Karen is now a part time receptionist (for the past 8 years) with Weight Watchers.

Contact us: If you have any questions we can answer, please don'thesitatetocallus.CoachBeaucanbereachedat beaujbrock@yahoo.com.